Living Alongside a Child's Recovery

Therapeutic Parenting with Traumatized Children

Billy Pughe and Terry Philpot

Foreword by Mary Walsh

Jessica Kingsley Publishers
London and Philadelphia

First published in 2007
by Jessica Kingsley Publishers
116 Pentonville Road
London N1 9JB, UK
and
400 Market Street, Suite 400
Philadelphia, PA 19106, USA

www.jkp.com

Library of Congress Cataloging in Publication Data

Pughe, Billy.
Living alongside a child's recovery : therapeutic parenting with traumatized children / Billy Pughe and
Terry Philpot ; foreword by Mary Walsh.
    p. cm.
Includes bibliographical references and index.
ISBN-13: 978-1-84310-328-8 (pbk. : alk. paper)
ISBN-10: 1-84310-328-1 (pbk. : alk. paper) 1. Psychic trauma in children--Treatment. 2. Child
psychotherapy--Parent participation. 3. Parenting. I. Philpot, Terry. II. Title.
[DNLM: 1. Child Abuse--therapy. 2. Stress Disorders, Post-Traumatic--therapy. 3. Parenting. 4. Child.
WS 350 P978L 2007]
RJ506.P66P84 2007
618.92'8914--dc22

2006032168

British Library Cataloguing in Publication Data

A CIP catalogue record for this book is available from the British Library

ISBN-13: 978 1 84310 328 1
ISBN-10: 1 84310 328 8

Printed and bound in Great Britain by
Athenaeum Press, Gateshead, Tyne and Wear

Books are to be returned on or before
the last date below.

Delivering Recovery

Series edited by Patrick Tomlinson, Director of Practice Development, SACCS

This is an essential series on practice for all professionals and parents involved in providing recovery for traumatized children and young people. Each book offers a practical and insightful introduction to an aspect of SACCS' unique and integrated approach to children traumatized by sexual, physical and emotional abuse.

also in the series

Reaching the Vulnerable Child
Therapy with Traumatized Children
Janie Rymaszewska and Terry Philpot
Foreword by Mary Walsh
ISBN-13: 978 1 84310 329 5   ISBN-10: 1 84310 329 X

The Child's Own Story
Life Story Work with Traumatized Children
Richard Rose and Terry Philpot
Foreword by Mary Walsh
ISBN-13: 978 1 84310 287 8   ISBN-10: 1 84310 287 0

of related interest

Therapeutic Approaches in Work with Traumatized Children and Young People
Theory and Practice
Patrick Tomlinson
Foreword by Paul van Heeswyk
ISBN-13: 978 1 84310 187 1   ISBN-10: 1 84310 187 4
Community, Culture and Change 14

Creative Therapies with Traumatized Children
Anne Bannister
ISBN-13: 978 1 84310 155 0   ISBN-10: 1 84310 155 6

Sexual Abuse
The Child's Voice – Poppies on the Rubbish Heap
Madge Bray
Introduction by Sarah Boyle
ISBN-13: 978 1 84310 487 0   ISBN-10: 1 84310 487 2

The Truth is Longer Than a Lie
Children's Experiences of Abuse and Professional Interventions
Neerosh Mudaly and Chris Goddard
ISBN-13: 978 1 84310 317 2   ISBN-10: 1 84310 317 6

To Michael and our son, Jaks, for their love
and encouragement, and to my parents with whom
my experience of parenting began.

Billy Pughe

Frances and Ernest Munting, always in mind

Terry Philpot

A Note and Acknowledgements

The names of all children and young people mentioned in this book have been changed, along with any details which might identify them.

As with the previous books in this series, for ease of reading we have referred to the children and young people as 'she' and all adults as 'he', except where, as in the case of a mother or other female adult, it has been necessary to be specific.

The outcomes on pages 112–18 were developed by Mary Walsh, chief executive, SACCS, and senior colleagues at SACCS.

We are grateful to Patrick Tomlinson, director of practice development, SACCS, for his oversight as the book progressed and his useful comments, and to Mary Walsh for her support.

We are especially grateful to the household managers within SACCS who through a series of practice workshops provided much of the practice material for the chapters; and to John Baker, deputy director of practice development, and Lorraine Easterbrook, deputy director, Shrewsbury region, SACCS, who supplied material for the case examples.

We should like also to thank Jessica Kingsley, managing director, Jessica Kingsley Publishers, and Steve Jones, commissioning editor, for their continuing help and support.

Contents

Foreword

When we started SACCS in 1987 we never thought that we would be offering residential care and treatment for traumatized children. In those early days we were developing and pioneering techniques to communicate with a very vulnerable group of children who had been sexually abused, usually in early childhood, specifically about their distress.

We worked with children from all over the country, and discovered that there were some very young children who because of their disturbed or eroticized behaviour were unable to be held in foster care. These children's placements broke down frequently, and eventually they were labelled as unfosterable and placed in residential care with adolescents on remand.

Our dream was to be able to safely hold those children and their behaviour lovingly whilst we worked therapeutically on the issues underlying their behaviour. This ambition was to become our first residential project which we called Leaps and Bounds. It took us until June 1991 to make it a reality, when our first house Hopscotch was opened.

Since then we have developed our services to meet the needs of these children, many of whom are emotionally fragmented. They are children who have suffered profound harm, have had multiple placement breakdowns, have had many losses in their young lives, and because of this have attachment disorders and unfortunately further abuse and damage through the care system. Both their internal and external worlds have been affected and we have developed services to help the whole child to recover. There are three strands to this important work: therapeutic parenting, therapy and life story.

This book is about therapeutic parenting, one of the most precious, valuable and responsible jobs, because if these children are not parented appropriately and well, they will struggle to effectively parent their own children.

Billy Pughe and Terry Philpot have written a comprehensive description of the SACCS approach to therapeutic parenting, and because of the integrated nature of our work, they have also referred to the other two strands, play therapy and life story work. They look at how physical, emotional and sexual abuse impacts on children's development and how attachment issues, separation, loss and the effects of trauma impact on the child's day-to-day care.

The therapeutic parenting team work closely with the therapist and life story worker, and together as the recovery team they hold the whole child, each part of the work informing the other. They are expected to tolerate the intolerable, to think about the unthinkable, to be with the youngsters in the deepest of distress. To hold each child in mind, which means that they are so attuned, they are aware of everything that has significance for the child, in the same way as a mother would in relation to her own child.

We believe that all children who have been emotionally injured through abuse should have the opportunity to recover from their injuries. When these injuries are profound they may need treatment outside of a family since because of their experience they may perceive a family to be one of the most dangerous places. I hope that this book will be a resource for all those caring for these children, and a reference for social workers and other professionals who are supporting them.

The child is always at the centre of everything that we do and I have great respect for the courage that each child shows on their painful journey back to emotional health. And that respect extends also to all those dedicated workers who accompany them, sharing their burden and easing their way.

Mary Walsh
Founder and Chief Executive of SACCS

Introduction

This is the third book in the Delivering Recovery series and, like its prede-
cessors, it is intended for those who work with children and young people
traumatized through abuse. We hope, though, that it will enjoy a reader-
ship wider than that because therapeutic parenting has much to tell us
about what constitutes good child care and how to work with all children.
It also throws considerable light on ideas about parenting. As Miller (1995)
says: 'The damage done to us in childhood cannot be undone because we
cannot change anything in our past. We can, however, change ourselves'
(p.28). For that change to take place great skill is needed on the part of practitioners and it is our intention to show how that skill is practised when it
comes to therapeutic parenting.

In Chapter 3, where we explain therapeutic parenting in some detail,
we quote Aynsley-Green (2005) as saying that nurture is now regarded as a
rather dated term as opposed to the modish 'parenting'. He makes a plea for
its restoration. Therapeutic parenting is very much about nurture, offering a
traumatized child, actually and symbolically, that care, attention and
nurture which she will have been denied in growing up. Nurture perhaps
too captures something of the idea of total care – physical and emotional –
which the good parent offers his child. To use another term, it looks to
Winnicott's 'maternal preoccupation'. But therapeutic parenting is more
than a replication of parental attitudes and actions. It is also informed by
psychodynamic theory and an understanding of attachment theory.

Children who have suffered early neglect and deprivation and the most
severe and continuing abuse will be left with critical gaps in their emotional
development. To say that therapeutic parenting seeks to fill the gaps seems

to suggest some kind of mechanistic approach. But what we are describing is about how filling those gaps restores the child's self.

Life story work and therapy, which were the subjects of the two earlier volumes in the series, are about working with children as individuals: the one helping them understand their biography as a means of understanding who they are and the world which has shaped them; the other a quest into the children's emotions and psyche to allow them to explore their experiences within the safety and containment of metaphor. Therapeutic parenting is also about working with children both as individuals and in a group. Children are born into families, good and bad, in which they learn about the world and judge and test themselves against other family members, their parents, as much as their brothers and sisters, if they have them. Thus, with therapeutic parenting the collective experiences of, say, mealtimes are as important as the individual experiences of, say, bathtime, going to bed and waking. How one's own bedroom is decorated says much to the individual child about how she is valued, but the state of the garden or the dining room says much to all the children in the house about how they are valued.

Put simply, therapeutic parenting is a way of compensating a child for what she was not offered by her parents or early carers. It does so in an atmosphere in which the child feels accepted and valued, where she feels loved and secure, protected and supported, and where the care she receives is consistent. It is what a good parent does, but whereas good parenting is spontaneous and 'natural', therapeutic parenting is, as we have said, a pro-fessional skill. It is applied to children who do not have the ease, self-confi-dence, self-esteem, spontaneity and openness of a healthy child. Thus, to be a therapeutic parent places great responsibility and resultant stress on the worker and this latter aspect is something which is also discussed.

Like the therapeutic community, whose influence in this area of practice is described, therapeutic parenting is practised in a total environment, physical and emotional, individual and group. Thereby, it challenges a child's distorted inner working model and, as Miller says, it literally changes the self.

CHAPTER 1

A Deep Wound

Abuse and its Effects on Traumatized Children

Since the 1980s child sexual abuse has become increasingly recognized. While it had not been previously ignored, the main emphasis had been first on neglect, which was the main reason why the great children's charities like Barnardo's, NCH (Philpot 1994; Wagner 1980) the Children's Charity and the NSPCC came into existence in the latter part of the nineteenth century. In more recent times, and particularly in the wake of the death of Maria Colwell in 1973 (Department of Health and Social Services 1974), the physical abuse of children again became the focus of professional, media and public attention. Very few children suffer only one kind of abuse and for too many children the three types go hand in hand. This book is largely concerned with children who have been traumatized because of sexual abuse, but it is safe to say that the overwhelming majority will have been physically and psychologically abused, as well as suffering from general neglect.[1]

How we understand sexual abuse is something that changes from culture to culture and from period to period. In mid-Victorian England the age of consent was 14. It still remains so in some countries or is even lower. In Chile and Mexico it is 12; in Spain, North Korea and South Korea it is 13; in Denmark, Sweden and France it is 15; in Northern Ireland (a part of the UK), New York and Bolivia it is 17; in California, Vietnam and Egypt it is 18; and in Tunisia it is 20 (*Guardian* 2005). In some African and Middle

Eastern countries female genital circumcision is considered acceptable practice. Although illegal in the US and UK, operations are still carried out in both those countries. In some parts of India a boy will be masturbated to 'make him manly' and a girl to 'make her sleep well'. In ancient Greece sexual relations between men and boys were accepted.

One of the most common forms of child abuse today is child prostitution. It is estimated that in the US there are 300,000 child prostitutes. In Thailand, with which it is more commonly associated, the estimate is 200,000. In Britain there are thought to be 5000 children in the sex trade and in France 8000 (Sanderson 2004). The development of technology has allowed abuse to become even more pervasive and in many ways less detectable: pornographic images of children can be displayed in the privacy of one's own home at the click of a button. So it is only slowly that more subtle forms of sexual abuse are being accepted as falling within that definition. Buying, selling or otherwise disseminating and obtaining pornographic videos, photographs, DVDs and films that feature children, sometimes no more than babies, is not a victimless crime.

The Department of Health (2003) defined child sexual abuse in a way that commands general support, albeit emphases differ. It said child abuse is:

> Forcing or enticing a child or young person to take part in sexual activities whether or not the child is aware of what is happening. The activities may involve physical contact, including penetrative (eg, rape or buggery) and non-penetrative acts. They may include non-contact activities such as involving children in looking at, or in the production of pornographic material, or watching sexual activities, or encouraging children to behave in sexually inappropriate ways.

This shows that the forms which abuse takes can vary greatly: with non-contact it can range from grooming children; from insisting on sexually seductive behaviour and dress to exposing a child to pornography and getting a child to recruit other children. Contact can include open-mouth kissing and sexual arousal to touching to rape and anal intercourse and oral sex. Sanderson (2004) offers a comprehensive list compiled from research into children's experiences. Babies as well as 15-year-olds are sexually abused.[2] The group estimated to be most at risk are children aged 5 to 12 years of age.

It is within the wider context of family dysfunction, privation and deprivation that abuse usually appears, although abuse may remain more easily hidden in 'respectable' middle-class homes where it is often assumed not likely to occur. The extent of abuse cannot be recorded with any certainty because, like adult rape, much goes unreported and may only be revealed when the victims are adults.

Both boys and girls are sexually abused, but girls are more commonly abused by a ratio of nearly 1:4 (ChildLine 2003).[3] Although abuse by people whom the child does not know tends to gain the headlines and provoke fears of 'stranger-danger', abusers are far more likely to be someone known to the child. This could be a family member or family friend, and this includes, of course, children who abuse other children. Abuse is also often systematic and continuing. It may last months or even years. Some children are abused into young adulthood and the abuse only ends when they leave the family home, although even that is sometimes not the case.

'Stranger-danger' is rare but commands front-page attention. So-called paedophile rings are another factor that gains much media attention. These rings, however, do often involve relatives as well as others not known to the child. As stated above, most abuse is committed by men against girls, but fathers can abuse sons and mothers their daughters and sons. Couples can jointly abuse their children, while women can also collude in abuse when they do not commit it.

Ordinary children, extraordinary lives

A child who has been abused is an ordinary child to whom extraordinarily damaging things have happened. Just as there is no such thing as a 'typical child', there is no such thing as a 'typical abused child'. Each child will react differently to her abuse, its effects and the trauma she suffers. All we can say in general is that abuse and its effects will be profoundly damaging.

Before we discuss these effects, it is important to remember that an abused child's perceptions of her abuse and other things may be very different from those who seek to help her. Alvarez (1992) makes a point worth bearing in mind when she states:

What the abuse has meant for him [sic] and meant to him may be very different from its meaning for us. He may, for example, be too emotionally and cognitively blunted for anything much to have any meaning at all. Or he may have been corrupted himself and have become fascinated with abuse or an abuser himself. He may fear the abuser far more than he fears the abuse. Or he may feel deep love for the abusing figure and this love may be stronger than his fear or distaste for the abuse. Or he may have all of these difficulties. In any case, our notions of protection, of justice, of care, may be quite unreal to him. (p.152)

Such situations present a child with desperate dilemmas and place her in a terrible double bind. She has disclosed abuse and is trying to make sense of the new chaos she feels enveloping her. She will be asking herself how she will defend herself from the wounding accusations which she will face from those affected by her allegation. The abuser, too, still dominates her world.

There are numerous consequences of disclosure for which the child will, quite naturally, feel she is responsible. For example, if the accused adult (who may well be the child's parent or grandparent) is found guilty by the court, the child will know that that person will go to prison. Because of her allegations, all or some of her brothers and sisters may go into care, while she herself may well be about to take the same route – a journey about which she is entirely ignorant and at best can only feel apprehensive about. There may be other forms of family disruption, conflict and disturbance. While some family members may feel sorry for her, want to help her and be glad that she had the courage to come forward, others – including some of her own brothers and sisters – may be divided about whether she should have made her allegations. They may not even believe her. Some may feel that she brought abuse on herself or that her allegations were malicious; that she is a liar or intrinsically bad.

As the trauma unfolds and the offender is brought to task, it is highly likely that at some point the child will again suffer great panic and fear. She may even question the wisdom of what she has done and has caused to happen. Was I to blame? What did I do to make Dad want to act sexually with me? Everything may appear to be out of control. She may wish she could go back in time and leave things as they were, coming to believe that bad as they were, things were not as bad as what is happening now.

Self-doubt or mounting confusion are now the child's companions and it is likely that she will condemn herself and question whether the abuse really warranted all the fuss and interference – was it *really* that bad? Did the abuse ever justify the dreadful drama of the courtroom and the consequences which flowed from it? She may well weigh in her mind whether her need to put a stop to the abuse is worth the events that follow: the family riven: she and her brothers and sisters in care, her father in prison, her mother alone.

The child can also come to the gradual realization that although she is now physically removed from the environment where she was abused, the trauma itself is just as raw. In essence, she may feel that she has not really escaped at all. Indeed, she could experience the outcome of a 'successful' conviction as having stumbled into what Hunter (2001) calls 'the sinking mud of despair' (p.79).

The child may now have greatly conflicting thoughts and feelings, enormously disrupted emotions, perhaps feeling one thing one moment and another the next. There also seems to be no way of knowing what was the right thing to do or anyone who can assure her that she can now be helped to move to a better life (whatever she is actually told). All of this makes the child see nothing but a precipice and below it a dark, unfathomable valley. To escape this, she may see the answer as the wish, the deep, deep desire, to succumb to the urge to go into emotional free-flow. She may crave to feel nothing at all, to become numb or able to switch off all the noise and for her world to fall silent. She may experience thoughts and sensations that appear to make her feel she is about to break into small pieces. She may feel the threat of annihilation, an almost literal sense of that 'going to pieces' that so many of us express as a feeling when things seem beyond our control. She lacks anchor, direction and any sense of grounding or rootedness. This wish to let go, to become as nothing, seems a way out.

A child like this is typical in the sense that she is one of those children whose physical and sexual abuse have been so severe and so brutal that a return home or a foster or adoptive placement are ruled out in the foreseeable future.

The abusing parent (most commonly the father) may go to prison and whatever stability there was (although many such children come from very unstable environments where adults come and go) may disappear. Children who make allegations of abuse rarely want their parents to be punished or understand that this could happen as a result of what they say. If a child who has been removed from the family home, or whose abuser is imprisoned, then experiences subsequent abuse, she may keep the secret to herself for fear that this will occasion more loss. What such children want is for the abuse to stop. They can have very complicated emotions, sometimes feeling both love and hate towards the abuser.

As we have said, many children who are abused live a very chaotic existence and a number of people will have come and gone in their lives. They may have only the vaguest understanding of who some of these people are, even if they are related.[4] The children may also have moved with bewildering rapidity from place to place.

The irony is that the care system, rather than offering stability, can often replicate children's sense of being permanently unsettled as they are moved from placement to placement. This increases the sense of their living what Hunter (2001) calls 'shattered, discontinuous lives [where] information about them becomes fragmented and lost' (p.26).

Rymaszewska and Philpot (2006) explain one important effect on these children's lives:

> Loss underpins many of the lives of these children. It is rather like the loss caused by death and, in some ways, children who suffer the terrible losses to which we refer here, react in the classic stages of those who are dying: denial and isolation; anger; bargaining; depression; and acceptance (Kubler-Ross 1970). However, while the stage of acceptance for a dying person is about allowing a 'good death', an acceptance that death is a part of life, not a violation of it, the child comes to acceptance of her loss in a more negative sense: she accepts that life has done what it has to her and the means of surviving that loss or dealing with it is to detach herself from others, not to expect good of people, to doubt their intentions, not to trust them. This can then be translated in many cases into anger, sadism, and a need for revenge. The model of the world that the child has arrived at is one that makes perfect emotional – and even intellectual – sense in the

light of what the world has done to her. Her world has been tipped upside down and she experiences her own perverse universe where love equals sex, hate equals love, sex and love both equal pain. She sees through a glass darkly. (p.33)

They add:

As a result of these distortions, children can become aggressive, detached and withdrawn, highly unpredictable in their behavior, and pre-programmed for failure. They can throw temper tantrums, kick, spit and bite. They are frequently self-destructive to the point where they can be suicidal. They may abscond, trash their homes, or steal. They may destroy the very things that are important to them. Their psychosexual development has been grossly distorted so that their behavior toward staff, foster carers, other children, and even complete strangers can be highly eroticized.

They are unable to trust people because it is safer not to do so. They have lost a sense of who they are and, in a literal sense, where they are. They can be driven by an abject terror of having to face the fact that no one wants them. They are, in their own eyes, thrown-away children. This may mean that they take control of their lives by ensuring that others cannot get close to them: they can act to ensure that there is no reason why they should be wanted. (p.34)

This, and the other consequences of what has happened to her, only depresses further a child's lack of self-worth, not to mention increasing her sense of confusion. One person for her becomes as good as another, however well meaning that person – social worker or foster carer – may be. Consequently there seems to be no point in investing in them emotionally because she believes, from past experience, that they will disappear like the last person. Even when a placement is permanent, it will take a long while for the child to come to accept this – after all, why should she?

The courts and criminal justice system can exacerbate the situation. For example, not only may a child have to appear in court and give evidence of the most traumatic kind, possibly against her parent, but sometimes she will have waited as long as 18 months before being called upon to do so. In interviewing 50 child witnesses, aged 7 to 17, 32 of them in sex offence cases, Plotnikoff and Wolfson (2005) discovered that children felt intimidated in court. Some said that appearing as a witness could be as traumatic as the original abuse. Just under half said that they had been accused of lying and more than half said that they had been very upset, distressed or angry. A fifth said that they had cried, felt sick or sweated.

A sense of loss and rejection, loneliness, having to rely on your own resources (meagre as these may seem) to do much about anything, an inability to trust others or feel that they are really there to help – these are the consequences of what abuse, the care and criminal justice systems and the courts bequeath to children who are abused. To this must be added the fact that abused children may develop a profound sense of their own badness. They may feel that they have deserved what happened to them, and this is something that will impinge on their sense of their own worth.

The physical act of moving from place to place, often with a changing cast of adults, has its emotional consequences in a sense of dislocation and rootlessness and the inability to form attachments. Without specialized and highly professionalized care such children, once out of the care system, can drift into unsatisfactory relationships, often replicating the violence and abuse which has blighted their own lives, or they can become prey again to violence and abuse as adults.

Exercises

1. Undertake a survey for a week of the daily papers and TV broadcasts.

2. Reflect on the incidents of reported sexual abuse: note the patterns and nature of the incidents and how they are reported.

3. What conclusions do you draw about the prevalence of abuse and society's view of it?

CHAPTER 2

Mind, Body and Soul
Attachment, the Brain, Trauma and Abuse

In the previous chapter we referred to some of the effects that abuse and the care system can have on children. However, because so much more is now understood about the effects of abuse so profound that the children require therapeutic intervention, it is worth devoting some attention to what therapeutic parenting is trying to deal with.

Attachment

Critical to understanding what therapeutic parenting seeks to do is attachment theory. In the 1950s, Bowlby (1969) developed the theory when explaining how patterns of behaviour either persist or change over time and across relationships. Howe (2000) explains attachment behaviour as: 'an instinctive biological drive that propels infants into protective proximity with their main carers whenever they experience anxiety, fear or distress' (p.26).

Bowlby (1969) said that we will develop maturely when our attachment stems from a nurturing and loving relationship. However, if our early relationship is based on violence, rejection, pain, abuse, lack of bonding and disruption, there will be problems such as in relationships with others and, in extreme cases, criminal, violent or abusive sexual behaviour. Elsewhere Bowlby (1979) explained:

Evidence is accumulating that human beings of all ages are happiest and able to deploy their talents to their best advantage when they are confident that standing behind them, there are one or more trusted persons who will come to their aid should difficulties arise. The person trusted, also known as an attachment figure, can be considered as providing his or her companion with a secure base from which to operate. (p.103)

Although the earliest writing on attachment emphasized the parent–child relationship (and this will remain the formative relationship for the overwhelming majority of children), it is now accepted that there are also other factors which can have an impact on our attachment. These include: infants being genetically vulnerable; trauma at and before birth; extended or repeated separation from the mother; undiagnosed, unrecognized or unresolved painful illness; frequent moves and placements; inconsistent or inadequate care; poor parenting; and parents who themselves have an attachment disorder (Adoption UK 2000, pp.24–25).

Being unattached to a parent does not necessarily mean that a child cannot form an attachment with someone else. For example, she may form a very strong attachment to her grandmother although she has a poor attachment with her mother (Lanyado 2000). Therapeutic parenting is based on the idea that children can be re-parented and thus form attachments, sometimes called 'secondary attachments' (Lanyado 2000), with professional caregivers.

The internal working model is the mechanism by which the child attempts to connect herself, other people and the relationship between them. The quality of the child's caring experiences will determine whether the internal working model is positive or negative. Children's adaptation to their internal working model can be one of:

- secure attachment (the carer is loving and the child is loved)

- ambivalence (the caregiver is inconsistent in how he responds and the child sees herself as dependent and poorly valued)

- avoidance (the caregiver is seen as consistently rejecting and the child is insecure but compulsively self-reliant)

- disorganized (caregivers are seen as frightening or frightened and the child is helpless, or angry and controlling) (Howe 2000, p.27).

Archer (2003) calls internal working models the 'road maps' that provide children with an internal framework of their world. According to Burnell and Archer (2003), the internal working models map out the most suitable response-routes to the familiar and unfamiliar:

> IWMs [internal working models] reflect the child's view of, and confidence in, the attachment figures' capacity to provide a safe and caring environment. Moreover, these models, in turn, organize the child's thoughts, memories and feelings regarding attachment figures. Inevitably, they will also act as guides and predictors of future behavior for the child and analogous attachment figures, such as adoptive parents. (p.65)

Schore (1994) refers to these models as being burned into the unconscious at the neurobiological level and Solomon and George (1999) say that once established they are highly resistant to change.

Loss can extend from the original object which is lost, say the parent, to the foster carer, social worker, friends and family. Children can become disengaged from school and the community. Those who experience a number of placements in care can undergo a double loss – the loss of individuals and also a loss of place as they may be situated hundreds of miles from their home, community and family.

In all of this both biology and the psyche are at work. Violence and abuse also interfere with the growth of the brain, which then can lead to various forms of disturbed behaviour. Even babies, according to YoungMinds (2004), can suffer mental health problems as a result of early abuse:

> Research strongly suggests that the way in which the brain develops is linked to early infant relationships, most often with the primary carer. Whilst other relationships in later life can be crucial, for example relationships with adoptive parents, these primary infant/carer relationships have a key impact on the mentally healthy development of the child... Active, satisfying and reciprocal relationships with parents create the basis for a sense of inner confidence and effectiveness. (p.1)

YoungMinds continues:

> There is evidence to suggest that the quality and content of the baby's relationship with his or her parents may affect the development of the neurobiological structure of the infant brain in a way that is harder to alter the longer the relationship patterns endure... Whilst we need to understand much more in this field, we are learning about serious, long-term consequences of neglect, trauma and abuse on early brain development and subsequent physical, emotional and social growth. (pp.1–2)

Such findings show that nurture and nature, rather than being mutually exclusive, are intertwined. But how is this? How does abuse affect the brain? How does trauma make itself felt on behaviour?

The structure of the brain

The brain is an immensely complex piece of machinery: it has over 100 billion brain cells or neurons, including glial and ganglia cells. Each neuron has, on average, 10,000 synapses or connections, which means that there are 1,000,000 connections between two brain cells and other brain cells (Cohen 2002). Cohen explains both the enormous importance and sensitivity of brain development:

> The brain starts to be identifiable when the foetus is three weeks old as a slab of cells in the upper part of the embryo. In the womb, the brain develops far more than other parts of the body. As a result, when babies are born, their heads are very large in relation to the rest of their bodies. Two-thirds of the brain is present at birth. In its structure and anatomy, the newborn baby's brain is remarkably like that of an adult.
>
> At birth, the baby will have all its 100 billion neural cells in the brain. More brain cells do not sprout until the baby is born and becomes able to see, move and speak. Missing at birth, however, are most of the connections between the cells.
>
> As the baby feels, moves and perceives, these connections are created. From the outset, heredity and environment interact. The baby's individual experiences create particular pathways and connections between particular cells. A baby brought up in a dark room does not form the pathways for normal vision, for example. (pp.14–15)

However, a baby's brain does not emerge fully formed at birth. As Cairns (2002) puts it: 'Once the baby is born, the real work of brain building begins'. Babies rely for their physical survival and growth on being fed and well cared for – something provided (for most children) by their parents. But also critical to healthy development is what their senses alert them to: soft words, warmth, and the feeling of being secure. Loving responsiveness to a baby's needs helps to build neural pathways in its brain. These pathways allow the baby to understand the way in which loving and healthy relationships work. But the baby who experiences the opposite – who is not held, hears only harsh words and noise, is moved suddenly, pushed, shoved or hit – becomes an anxious, stressful and fearful child.

Thus, the brain is much more than an extraordinary computer or a library of unquantifiable knowledge. It also allows us from our very earliest existence to receive messages, to take in the world and how we perceive it and what it is telling us. In short, it is the vehicle by which we learn, even as babies, how to become social beings. Even in the womb, a baby picks up its mother's moods or the experience a mother may be having (say, domestic abuse). The brain as well as the body reacts: the foetus can be damaged by drinking, smoking, drug taking (even of prescribed drugs), or prenatal mal-nutrition. The growth of brain cells can be negatively affected. According to Cairns (2002):

> Attachment behaviours are the key to this early infant brain develop-ment. Stress is toxic to the brain, causing profound changes in the brain structure and function in the interests of survival. When the baby attempts to engage the caregiver through attachment behaviour, the urgent desire is for the caregiver to enable the baby to modulate and recover from the stress which has provoked the behaviour. Babies with available and responsive caregivers enter into a relationship in which each attunes to the other and together they experience relief of stress. Both baby and caregiver will go through a cycle of stress arousal, stress modulation and the pleasurable experience which follows the soothing of stress. Most babies (55–70 per cent) are fortunate enough to have such a relationship with their caregiver. (p.49)

Where there is positive parenting, at 24 weeks' gestation 124 million con-nections can be found on brain tissue the size of a pinhead (Karr-Morse and Wiley 1997). At birth there are 253 million connections and by eight months the number could be 572 million. Thus, by eight months of age the baby's brain has produced the maximum capacity for versatility and flexibility and this number of connections is more than is needed.

But what happens to the brain when parenting is negative? Cairns (2002) shows that some brain connections are not produced and 'pruning' of those already there but unused takes place when there is negative or poor stimulation of the child by the parent. She goes on to say that there is a 'qualitative difference' between the brains of securely and insecurely attached children. Securely attached children develop bigger brains. She adds:

> Confronted with persistent unresolved stress, the infant brain forms characteristic use-dependent structures, of either hyper-arousal or defensive dissociation: hyper-aroused infants show perpetual signs of distress and irritability, while dissociated infants show none despite being in a physiological state of high arousal. (Cairns 2002, p.50)

It can be seen, therefore, that neural pathways can be affected by a range of subtle and not so subtle influences, positive and negative.

The effects of trauma on the brain

What is trauma? Ziegler (2002) states: 'Anything that disrupts the optimal development of a child can be defined as a type of trauma to the system.' (p.35) This takes in both pre-birth and post-birth experiences and even birth itself. Ziegler tells us that 'the most serious finding' of the past decade is that neglect has the most long-lasting effect on the development of the brain and is the 'most persistent and pervasive' form of trauma. He goes on:

> The concern is not only how the brain reacts to neglect as a threat to survival, but also what the brain is not doing while preoccupied in survival mode. Neglect shifts the focus of the infant away from the exploration and essential learning the brain is prepared to do at the beginning of life. (p.37)

Some kinds of trauma affect some children in different ways, depending on the type of trauma, the age of the child and the circumstances she was in at the time it happened. James (1994) describes trauma as 'an actual or perceived threat of a danger [which] overwhelms a person's usual coping ability' (p.10). Trauma can overwhelm so that what comes in its wake can appear to be uncontrollable, leaving us, as James says, feeling, 'literally, helpless, vulnerable to the point of a fear for one's self, [experiencing] a loss of safety so that one feels wary of others, and loss of control so that one's actions become unpredictable' (p.11).

Trauma can affect a child's sense of identity, development, trust in others, her ability to manage her behaviour, and so on. For a child, trauma is very likely to be much more far-reaching than for an adult and may seriously affect general social and individual functioning.

Lisa: The little girl who became someone else

Lisa was only four weeks old when, severely neglected, she was removed from the care of her parents and placed for adoption. However, she went into hospital because of her failure to thrive. She was then placed with foster carers with a view to being adopted at a later date, but 18 months later she displayed a marked change in behaviour with which the foster family had difficulty in coping. Although it was suspected that the foster carer's son was abusing her, she stayed with the family for another 18 months.

From then until she was 15 years old Lisa had no contact with her birth parents or her extended family. Lisa was again placed for adoption. The couple that came forward were friends of the social worker. They fostered Lisa and, during an unauthorized process prior to adoption (which did not take place), changed her name to Naomi. At three and a half Lisa no longer existed: her name was changed and her identity lost.

During the four years she spent with this foster family she was excluded from nurseries. Her difficult behaviour continued and became more pronounced. Lisa (now Naomi) was sexualized and aggressive toward children and adults; she drew pictures of male genitalia at nursery school. She inserted things into herself and encouraged others to do the same. The placement eventually broke down and Lisa was placed in a series of local authority children's homes where she was sexually abused by other residents.

When in another placement with much older female residents, she put tomato ketchup in her pants to simulate periods. Her desperate need to be the same as the others, to gain attention and status, due to having little sense of her own self and wanting in some way to protect herself from ridicule, led her into further abusive situations.

Lisa was finally placed in a therapeutic environment where her carer began the slow process of building an attachment and trying to make sense of her life. The need was to put her life in reverse in order to explain how she had come to be who she was. It was evident that Lisa needed to experience appropriate care, nurture, respect and love. She needed to know what it was like to be at the centre of healthy attention, to be thought about, and to be allowed to regress to enable the internal baby to experience a sense of total dependency on her carer.

The carer was able to do this by ensuring that Lisa's world became consistent, predictable and safe. Her routines were planned in detail with her. She was brought a full wardrobe of new clothes. She was washed and dressed and her clothes were laid out for her every day. Her hair, nails and teeth were given special attention. When she could not contain her anxieties of fear and distrust and had to be physically held by the adults, they did so while talking to her soothingly and calmly, demonstrating their ability to keep her safe and not be overwhelmed by her anger and violence.

This positive attachment with her carer enabled Lisa to make a healthy choice about who she wanted to be and, most fundamentally, what name she wanted to be known by. Over several years of painstakingly slow progress the child's carer was able to take Naomi back to being Lisa and to introduce her to her birth parents, her sister, grandparents and extended family. She had established an identity. She is Lisa.

Children will revert to a state of helplessness when traumatized. Like adults, they can adopt adaptive responses so that, for example, they avoid intimacy, feel that they need to be in control and act in ways that deter rela-tionships and closeness with others. They can experience flashbacks, hyperactivity and dissociation. These symptoms can affect their education and lead them to be diagnosed with various behavioural disorders. Depending on their age, they may turn to drugs and alcohol abuse and engage in promiscuous sexual relationships.

James (1994) states that the four major effects of trauma on children are a persistent state of fear, disordered memory, avoidance of intimacy and 'dysregulation of affect'. When emotions seem out of control, the person may feel that she is about to burst with emotion that would overwhelm herself and others, if allowed to do so. For children, this can show itself in play by fantasy, movement, speaking almost in voices, together with uncontrolled emotional outbursts unrelated to the play. Children can also exhibit this 'dysregulation of affect' by being defiant, anxious, unco-operative, depressed, impulse-ridden, acting unpredictably and being oppositional.

Trauma can also produce dissociation. A person may show an absence of emotion or appropriate emotion about painful and traumatic events. It is something which children commonly resort to in the absence of their ability to flee, when the strategy for flight consists of tantrums and aggres-sive behaviour.

Freezing can occur when something seems to threaten the child, allowing her to take it in and try to work out what to do. It can show itself in the child being oppositional-defiant. This is a conduct disorder when negative, defiant, disobedient or hostile behaviour is shown toward authority figures. Common signs and symptoms are temper tantrums, arguing with adults, actively defying rules, deliberately annoying people, unfairly blaming others for mistakes or misbehaviour, and being tetchy or easily annoyed, angry, resentful, spiteful or vindictive.

The trauma bond

Trauma can be deceptive. It may have the semblance of a secure attachment within a family. The two differ in that attachment is based on love while the trauma bond is based on fear and distorts the child's perceptions. She lives in a state of underlying uncertainty, dependence and apprehension and so seeks to appease the abuser, to serve or even anticipate his needs and demands. Children affected by the trauma bond will exhibit behaviour that is geared to meeting the stated needs of the adult or what she perceives those needs to be.

This can create a blueprint for future relationships, suggesting that they are best conducted by being servile and dependent. As she grows, a child can develop a victim mentality. She can become attracted to and invite relationships with powerful people who may cause harm and help to reinforce the blueprint. For adults, the trauma bond can influence how they see themselves as parents. Ziegler (2002) explains the apparent contradiction of the trauma bond:

> It may seem strange to say that survival can be promoted in negative ways, but this idea is the reality for many abused children. These children develop negative bonds that promote their survival, which are called loyalty bonds or trauma bonds. If someone holds your life in their hands, they are very relevant and powerful to you. Pleasing such a person, or at least not displeasing them, becomes critical. Such an experience can rapidly change an individual in lasting ways. The rape victim, the prisoner of war, the hostage, and the abused child all have similar experiences. (p.84)

For many children trauma may not seem unusual because of the experiences they have suffered almost before being conscious of them. Even when the experience is over, they may not realize this so what caused the trauma and its effects will, of course, still be with them. Thus, their loyalty continues and their trauma bonding stays with them, though the events which threatened them are over.

Exercises

1. Reflecting on a point made by Bowlby (1979), do you agree that you are happiest and achieve more when you feel supported by a significant other?

2. Try to recall significant events and achievements in your life.

3. Were there attachment figures that supported you?

4. What do you think would have been different if they had not been there?

5. Write five sentences which you believe describe your internal working model.

CHAPTER 3

Another Kind of Parent
What is Therapeutic Parenting?

Good parenting – loving, nurturing, secure, consistent, protective and supportive – is the cornerstone for any child's future healthy growth. How we develop as human beings – with warmth or coldness, openness or secretiveness, generosity or meanness of spirit – is determined by how we are treated as children. While Philip Larkin's pessimistic view of our parents can be sadly true in some instances, the opposite is also the case: when they mean to, your mum and dad, they help you grow. This occurs not merely from the first moments of life, when the newborn baby is placed in the security and warmth of its mother's embrace, but even before birth. The mother's experiences of anxiety, anger or tension can negatively influence the unborn child's growth, as can, more seriously, any experience of violence or trauma. Thus, the child whose parents look forward lovingly and positively to her birth, whose mother is calm and happy with her pregnancy and who feels herself to be part of a loving relationship, has a head start before she even leaves the womb.

Nurture, as Aynsley-Green (2005) has remarked, is a somewhat old-fashioned word not commonly used, but it is much more expressive of what a child needs for healthy growth than the more modish and neutral 'parenting'. Aynsley-Green lists the eight components of nurture as:

- love and care
- physical contact and comfort
- nutrition, warmth and protection from home

- security and stability
- play and exploration
- education
- friendships
- expectations and a purpose in life.

However, many children are denied such nurturing. In the most extreme cases, there are children, like those whose experiences are the basis of this book, who have been so severely abused, their emotional development so disrupted and their ability to make relationships with others so grossly impaired that they lack attachment. The majority of children who have been abused will not have received the emotional and physical nurture necessary for their development. Such deprivation and early neglect will have left them with critical gaps in their emotional development. They may be left emotionally frozen or fragmented, and have an inner working model which severely impairs their ability to form healthy attachments. For such children, critical to their recovery is the concept of therapeutic parenting.

Some of what underpins therapeutic parenting is described by Maginn (2006) when he writes of the need for a psychology-driven, practical approach to bettering outcomes for children and young people in care. He makes a helpful distinction between 'caring for a child' and 'caring about a child' and then goes on to say:

> When we learn this difference and have policies and standards that support 'caring about' activities, improvements in outcome may follow. By unpacking and analyzing the principles of 'good parenting' we can begin to ensure that children in public care will be brought up in an environment that enhances their development. (p.37)

Maginn has developed what he calls seven 'pillars of parenting' for those who work with children and young people in care. These 'pillars' fit very well with the idea of therapeutic parenting. They are:

- primary care and protection
- secure attachment
- positive self-perception
- emotional competence

- self-management skills
- resilience
- a sense of belonging.

For each pillar Maginn has devised the kind of supports which staff must offer. He then goes on to say:

> We don't expect professional child carers to achieve the 'unconditional love' that some children enjoy in highly functional families, but by incorporating the pillars of parenting into their work, carers and children can begin to share the experience of 'authentic warmth'. (p.37)

Therapeutic parenting is founded upon the principles of 'good parenting', or indeed 'ideal parenting'. There are, of course, other forms of alternative parenting to assist children whose lives suffer disruption, the most obvious being adoption and fostering. Fostering, particularly, can be used when a child's parents are temporarily unable to care for her, perhaps through illness or other personal difficulty. However, alongside 'good parenting' principles, therapeutic parenting is underpinned by psychodynamic theories of child development and an understanding of attachment theory. Such parenting offers the child, directly or indirectly, symbolically or actually, important experiences denied by his or her own natural parenting. It is offered within a substitute environment which must be safe and which the child must be able to trust. The kind of child to whom we are referring will need this specialist treatment before she is able to reach a point in her recovery which will enable her to be parented within a family.

Dockar-Drysdale (1990b) makes a distinction between good child care and the preoccupation of the ordinary devoted mother. What she calls therapeutic management is different again, although having much in common with maternal primary preoccupation. In later chapters, we shall discuss in detail the therapeutic significance of food, mealtimes and bedtimes, but it is useful to quote these two examples of everyday life which Dockar-Drysdale uses to show how child care and therapeutic involvement differ. She says that child care workers know a lot about food and just what children need to keep them well but she goes on: 'Therapeutic workers in residential work, while aiming to provide a balanced diet, are tuned to the emotional needs of the child where food is under consideration' (p.8).

She gives an example of children getting out of bed: 'I am sure that all child care workers are warm and friendly to the children they are waking. However, it is unlikely that they will use techniques which then will be faithfully employed by other people' (p.8). She goes on to offer the case of the 15-year-old who needed to have his forehead wiped with cool water and a little sponge. Then there was the other 15-year-old who liked to have his hand held while the person waking him talked softly. There were children who needed to be given a long time to wake up and not hurried; at times they would stay in bed and rise much later.

Elsewhere, Dockar-Drysdale (1968) talks about ten-year-old Marguerite, with whom she was walking in the street:

> Just at this moment she was emotionally exhausted and in the deepest part of a localized regression in which she was involved with me. I remember thinking, 'If she were really a baby, I'd pick her up and carry her home – as it is, what should I do?' As if in answer to my thoughts, Marguerite laid her hand in mine in a way that made it clear that in carrying her hand I would be carrying Marguerite herself. In this way she made it possible for me to provide the necessary experience. (p.102)

Whoever is the primary carer of a child who has been abused or maltreated – mother, father, other relatives, foster carer, adoptive parent, or key carer in residential care – needs to be consistently thoughtful about what a child is communicating through the way she behaves. An adult can respond helpfully in a manner that challenges a negative inner working model and defences so that the inner working model can be restructured. In doing so, the child is being 'told' that adults can be people who care and offer protection and that relationships need not necessarily be abusive ones. If this is not done, then the mistakes of past relationships are repeated. Foster care breakdown can occur not because the carer is negative toward the child but because he does not have the support which can occur in group settings.

Therapeutic parenting is needed when the developmental disruption which the child has experienced is severe. Then she has to be helped, by structured means, to move from insecure to secure attachment.[5] In these circumstances, therapeutic parenting seeks to compensate the children for deficiencies in their parenting with a regime that is accepting and containing and offers them the love, nurture, security, protection, consistency and support that they have not previously received.

These children are being 're-parented'. Good parents often tend to act spontaneously in caring for their children – that's a natural way of acting as a parent. Therapeutic parenting is a professional technique and, as such, is structured in the help that it offers, while giving as near as possible an approximation to the kind of positive parenting which a child should have received. Therapeutic parenting is partly about the creation of a physical environment that would be found in an ordinary home and the kind of care that the 'good' parent would have given to the child. The team of carers who work in the home carry out the task of therapeutic parenting. As Cairns (2002) puts it:

> All those who have made a commitment to the child now have to work together to construct an environment which will enable the child to move together from the cold and lonely wasteland of unmet attach-ment needs to the warmth and safety and supportiveness of secure attachment relationships.
>
> This environment must meet both the need for affective attunement and the need for reintegrative shame. It will be an environ-ment in which those close to the child are adopting a consistent approach which meets the child's needs, adapting the approach to fit their own role with the child but proving great consistency in the structures surrounding the child. (p.70)

She goes on to say that it is an environment where the child's individuality and uniqueness are respected, where she has certain inalienable rights, and which assumes that the child is a sociable and lovable being and that she will be able to discover that sociable and lovable nature if freed from anxiety and shame.

Jackie: A sense of abandonment

When Jackie's mother went out at night, there was no one to comfort her. If her mother returned, it would be with different people and she'd usually be drunk or in a drug-induced state. When she needed a fix, Jackie became a commodity for others to abuse to meet her mother's needs.

Jackie's feelings of being uncared for and left by her mother confirmed her sense of abandonment. This was manifested in her inability to accept that those with whom she was placed could and would care for her and that her welfare was important and worthwhile to them. She would become extremely anxious if the carer she was with temporarily left her. For example, if he went to the toilet Jackie would be outside the door; if he went to the office she would be there waiting. She became distressed and destructive if her carer was not at work that day, believing that he had left her forever.

To help her overcome her desperation, the containment offered had to be consistent, reliable and structured. She would be constantly reminded of what was planned for that day and who would be working with her. If it was known in advance (as was usually the case) that her key carer would not be available, then Jackie was told this and given the chance to express her fears and be reassured. She would be told when he was to return by making use of calendars and being reminded of events that had occurred on certain days so that she had a sense of how long it would be before he came back.

If his time away was an extended one, like a holiday, then he would send her a postcard or send or leave a letter for another carer to read. The key carer would telephone her at a given time to show that he was still thinking about her and was concerned for her, though physically absent. When he returned he might bring her a small gift, another token that she had been thought about and not forgotten in his absence.

Jackie had always to be aware of who was available to her, who would be putting her to bed and getting her up, and who would be preparing her food, getting her clothes ready. All of this reinforced the symbolism of the mother being preoccupied with her child.

The psychodynamic approach

Before saying more about therapeutic parenting, it is useful to offer a short explanation of the psychodynamic model of human development to which it is linked. Bateman, Brown and Pedder (2000) make a very obvious but useful distinction between behaviourist and psychodynamic approaches. The former, they state, studies the patient from the outside, being interested in the observable, the external, and preferably scientifically measurable behaviour. Whereas for the latter:

> The dynamic psychotherapist is more concerned to approach the patient empathetically from the inside in order to help him identify and understand what is happening in his inner world, in relation to his background, upbringing and development; in other words to fulfil the ancient Delphic injunction 'Know thyself'. (p.2)

Dynamic psychotherapy has evolved from Freudian and Jungian psychoanalysis. Its later application for children was developed by Anna Freud, Melanie Klein and Donald Winnicott. It has also been refined and added to by others such as Bowlby (1973–1980). Bowlby challenged Freud's understanding of anger as a response to loss (important when thinking about the children we are referring to). For Bowlby anger was part of a grief reaction, not a sign of pathological mourning (Preston-Shoot and Agass 1990).

Freud himself revised his theories and others have since given them further refinement. However, the idea that we are driven by unconscious motives, that our internal life can be as powerful as anything external, while not original to Freud (it can be found in writers and philosophers going back centuries), is his contribution to modern-day thought and clinical practice. He 'brought a mixture of courage, imagination and rigor to the task which took him into new territory' (Preston-Shoot and Agass 1990) and linked the concept of the life of the unconscious to a medical context, produced evidence from his clinical work and constructed a theory (Bateman *et al.* 2000). Thus, today we recognize that symptoms and forms of behaviour are a sign of the sometimes unconscious effects of our experiences. What troubles us can be denied or suppressed, but if this occurs then the effect of these experiences can be expressed in other ways that are damaging to ourselves and others. Preston-Shoot and Agass (1990) explain:

> Freud's concept of the unconscious is dynamic. It is pictured as an arena in which quantities of energy are constantly on the move, a

seething cauldron of raw emotion and irrationality. In keeping with the scientific orthodoxy of its day, it is also a biological concept, in that the psychic energy is fuelled by bodily drives. (p.19)

Even in Freud's day there were breaks within the movement (significantly, his splits with Alfred Adler and Carl Jung) and since then many other schools of dynamic psychotherapy have arisen. The words 'therapy' and 'psychotherapy' have thus found themselves appended to a variety of approaches, among them group, family, couple, social, gestalt and primal. However, all would agree on some common ground that derives from the idea that feelings and reactions of which we are not consciously aware and experiences long past can cause suffering in the present; and that such suffering can only be relieved if these are understood and consciously considered and addressed.

In referring to these many strands or schools, all of which are said to be 'psychodynamic', Leiper and Maltby (2004) talk of 'a tradition of developing ideas: a broad river, with a variety of channels and cross-currents' (p.12). Within this often-changing theoretical environment there are shared values and core ideas, the 'most fundamental' of which they sum up as:

the focus on psychological or emotional pain – often thought of as anxiety and conceptualized in terms of internal conflict – but most fundamentally, simply pain. Life is thought of as a difficult and demanding process and the psyche is built and continues to struggle to deal with it. What is 'dynamic' is the turbulence created in the currents of mental life by these struggles. (p.13)

They go on to say that psychodynamics can be defined 'in terms of the *process* of therapeutic change' [our italics] (p.13).

What does the psychodynamic approach say about children whose experiences are both different from those of adults but which can also carry on into adulthood? There are different schools of thought that began, famously, with Freud's theory of childhood sexuality. Others, notably Erikson (1950), have developed this. The non-dogmatic approach sums up an almost universally understood principle based on the psychodynamic perspective: that the problems we suffer as adults very often stem from the difficulties we have undergone as children, which can be part of the continuum from disturbance in childhood. Although some experiences more commonly occur when we are adults (say, for example, the effects of bereavement), it is really in infancy and childhood that we seek gratification of our basic needs – for love, care, security, and so on – by those closest to us, like our parents and other caregivers and our brothers and sisters. Where those needs have not been met, then our development can be limited and, in some cases, profoundly so.

In working with children, dynamics occur which can be understood better through knowledge of concepts such as transference, countertransference, defence mechanisms and attachment. These concepts are not, of course, exclusive to work with children. They can also be helpful when working with adults with, say, bereavement or relationship problems.

The person who perhaps contributed most to psychodynamic work with children was Donald Winnicott, the paediatrician and psychoanalyst. In his study of the development of infants, he was especially concerned with the way in which children's relationships with their parent or parents enabled them to move from absolute dependency toward physical and emotional independence. The mother, according to Winnicott, 'holds' the child literally, but she also holds the child's feelings metaphorically. Through this process the child comes to see herself as an individual in relation to others (Ward 2003). Parallel to this, Bowlby (1973–1980) was developing his theory of attachment, which we have discussed in detail in Chapter 2.

Schmidt Neven (1997) describes the following as some of the key components of the psychodynamic approach. However, as will become evident in this book, such components are key to the concept and practice of therapeutic parenting:

> All behavior has meaning – behavior is always a communication between children and parents.
>
> The child exists in the parent, and the parent exists in the child – the events surrounding our infancy and childhood shape our future.
>
> Behavior is dynamic and changes all the time – it is not static. The tension and interplay between our inner world and our outer world.
>
> The Overt and the Covert in our behavior. (p.4)

The origins of therapeutic parenting

As we have said, because of abuse some children's experiences have been so grossly negative that their development is impaired. This is when therapeutic parenting is used to 're-parent them', to give them a new start, via a new relationship akin to the positive parenting and home life which they have been denied.

Earlier we outlined some of the history behind the theories underpinning therapeutic parenting. It is, however, difficult to be certain as to where the model was first practised in the treatment of traumatized children. Many of the key elements can be seen in the writings of leading practitioners and consultants within residential child care and the therapeutic community movement.

The movement itself is not always easy to define because, as Kennard (1998) shows, the term 'therapeutic community' has been used to describe a series of not always obviously related institutions from prisons to long-stay hospitals, from residential care for children to centres for those with drug and alcohol problems. Including services for adults, children and young people, such communities also display different characteristics, which Kennard has tabulated (p.114). Only some of these characteristics may have any bearing on therapeutic parenting but, as Kennard remarks, they may be present in non-therapeutic establishments like schools. So far as therapeutic parenting is concerned, one would not, for example, expect it to embrace flattened hierarchies and the sharing of tasks – often in children's establishments devolving to children some tasks which would normally be those of the adult – or 'intimate and informal sharing of information among all members of the group'; or participating together in a range of purposeful tasks – therapeutic, domestic, organizational and educational.

However, therapeutic communities do offer a therapeutic environment, which is something else they have in common with therapeutic parenting. This is true both in the emotional and physical sense, as will be seen in Chapter 5 when we discuss the kind of physical surroundings conducive to children's recovery. Referring to therapeutic communities and therapeutic settings, Lanyado (2003) could easily be referring specifically to therapeutic parenting when she talks of nurturing environments for severely deprived children and their families being:

like taking the tender seedling and replanting it in a place where it has a better chance of growing. This is an enormously difficult and demanding task, as these children and their families require an emotional and physical caring equivalent to 'intensive care' if they are to recover. Attention to detail in their everyday lives is vital in bringing about this rehabilitation and is an essential aspect of the care that is provided in all good therapeutic environments. (pp.66–67)

It is also the case that some environments for children, while not therapeutic communities, have been informed by a psychotherapeutic understanding. One such is Summerhill, the 'free school' founded by A.S. Neill which continues to flourish. Although Neill was very much taken with the ideas of Freud, as was his American mentor, Homer Lane, at the Little Commonwealth, Neill complained that too many parents dumped problem children on him.[6]

When characterizing therapeutic communities, Kennard (1998) also lists 'a living learning situation' (p.114). This, he says, is 'a shared commitment to [another of his characteristics] the goal of learning from the experience and/or working together' (p.114). While it is not something associated with therapeutic parenting, we can see in 'living/learning' another of its ideals. After all, for most of us healthy development depends on what we learn in our own families: how we live with other people, how we learn to relate to them, how we learn to negotiate and accept the limitations on our own actions, and come to understand about those of others as they affect us.

Therapeutic parenting is more than about what we do for and with a child, just as ordinary parenting is. Children learn from their parents: what happens in 'our home' is regarded as a norm; how our parents act is implicitly the way we feel we should act. Much of what we learn, we learn by example. Canham (1998) considers the effect of the total atmosphere when he points out that it is not just the parental figures in residential homes to whom children turn for role models, 'but the whole way the organization functions is the basis for the possibility of an introjective identification.[7] It is perhaps useful to see the building itself and the systems that take place within it, as well as the staff, as a parental figure' (p.69). He goes on:

> Children and young people identify with and introject the institution they live in and the people who work in it. If they introject an organization capable of continuing to think about painful issues then they are more likely to develop this capacity themselves. Without the experience of this kind of processing, children and adolescents are unlikely to be able to relate to their own experiences and present and future relationships are likely to be contaminated by what has happened in the past. (p.69)

By implication, Rose (2002) sums up how therapeutic communities have influenced therapeutic parenting when he notes that the former have influenced many other psychosocial methods of treatment and goes on:

> Yet what will have mattered most to patients, especially in a residential context, is not so much the particular therapy, or even the staff's hard-won professional status, so much as their feeling that their *daily experience was consistently being made relevant to their real psycho-social needs.* (our italics; p.176)

This is the very essence of therapeutic parenting because, like the therapeutic community, the environment is constructed to be therapeutic. What happens there, the quality of the relationships, the physical attributes of the venue – these are intended to help, to be therapeutic, to replicate what the child has lost or never had. All are to aid the process of recovery. It is, as Rose adds, 'the capacity of the residential setting to generate healing and growth despite the residents' severe emotional problems' (p.184). It is 'an auspicious opportunity for those deprived of the emotional building blocks of self, whether this has existed since their emotionally deprived infancy, or as a consequence of specific unresolved psychological trauma' (Rose 2002, p.176).

Experience and engagement

Therapeutic parenting offers a child symbolic and actual experiences which seek to fill the gaps in her development. This simple statement disguises what this book will show: how the total effort and total environment – through care, personal interactions, how food is served and mealtimes conducted, myriad day-to-day activities, and so on – restore to the child her sense of self and identity because this provision challenges the child's negative inner working model and enables her to begin to feel differently about herself, other people and the world around her.

The word 'experiences' is important. Rose (1987) says it is about engagement in the process itself:

> It is not a memory jogger, for no one can remember what they have never experienced. The resident [of the therapeutic community] is never simply a passive recipient. He must play his part in the process and thus receive the nourishing consequences. The results of his con-tinually repeated engagement in the giving and receiving of nourish-ment [here Rose is referring specifically to food in the process] is that, like the fortunate baby, he can at last begin to perceive of himself as worthy to be fed and to give pleasure in return. (pp.160–161)

Rose refers to 'the fortunate baby' because he is writing about the experi-ences of adolescents, but the *experience* of therapeutic parenting is one which is available to children and adolescents who, in their own ways, can participate. Therapeutic parenting is not a passive activity: it is about group and one-to-one relationships, the acts of giving and receiving, and what that may positively lead to.

Therapeutic parenting is about the chance for each child to develop a primary attachment with one person, their key carer, which itself helps the child to develop her sense of self and her growing understanding of the needs of others and how she impacts on them. It is through this attachment that a child will be able to experience a level of preoccupation, akin to maternal preoccupation normally associated with infancy, through which her recovery can take place. With the support of the recovery team, the job of the key carer is to ensure that all the child's physical, emotional and ther-apeutic needs are met. Maternal preoccupation is when the therapeutic parent replicates, sometimes actually and at other times symbolically, the preoccupation which the mother gives to her child: that complete concen-tration on the child's every need.

Somewhat further along the path to recovery is the child's growing understanding that she lives in a community: there are others who have needs, just as she has, and part of this is the need to encourage her sense of empathy. This is partly done by holding children's meetings, which allow children to express their views and have them taken into account while learning about problem solving and how we interact with others. (The therapeutic and practical role of the group meeting is discussed in more detail in Chapter 5.)

Through internalizing their attachments and the experiences that children undergo in an accepting environment and through therapeutic parenting, they are able to reach a level of recovery which enables them eventually to move successfully on to family placement and to achieve their potential.

We can be harsh or considerate with children, reason with them or order them about, shout at them or speak softly, meet their needs or ours, provide for them or leave them to want. But it is not only how we treat children that influences them negatively or positively and allows them to draw inferences about how others regard them. It is also in the physical surroundings they are offered. Thus, the physical environment of therapeutic parenting is as important as the emotional atmosphere in which the child lives and the relationships which she enjoys.

Chapter 5 discusses at greater length how therapeutic parenting shows itself in a child's physical surroundings, but it is the case that the physical circumstances and surroundings of where the child lives are in themselves a therapeutic opportunity. It is one which is psychically, as well as physically, significant. It is specifically designed to meet the needs of the children. There is a total effort concentrated on the child in the total environment in which the child now finds herself. This is because every part of a child's life is seen as having a potential for therapy. Therefore, the home is structured in such a way that the everyday details reflect this.

Exercises

1. Reflect upon your own experiences of being parented.

2. List the key things that you feel made this experience positive.

3. Were there things that made the experience less positive?

CHAPTER 4

The Adult's World
Consultancy and Supervision

There are few if any other areas of work where compassion and anger, hope and desperation can so readily coexist as in work with children, the more so perhaps with those who have been traumatized through abuse. All children can often provoke very primitive feelings, both negative and positive, in adults. Something of this is to do with the fact that childhood is the one experience we have all been through and we all know (or think we remember) what it is like. In our contacts with children, whether we are professionally or personally responsible for them, comparisons with how we were treated and how our parents reacted to us or how we came to understand the wider world are natural and inevitable.

Even the parents of healthy children can sometimes feel that they are engaged in an uphill task and the most mature parents will sometimes seek help, if only from their own parents or friends. But those who work with traumatized children can frequently find the experience overwhelming, battering and exhausting. The sheer scale of the task before them, as well as the evocation of their feelings, can lead to burnout. This is why the type of organization in which therapeutic work takes place and the sort of support offered to practitioners are so critical to effective therapeutic parenting. A transparent organizational structure, an established organizational culture, clear role and task definitions, lines of accountability and appropriateness of authority to carry out the task are the context for the work, the framework of containment in which it is enabled to take place successfully.

As Butlin (1973) reminds us: 'You can have management without therapy but you can't have therapy without management.' As Ward *et al.* (2003) stress in relation to therapeutic practice, at its best it is a 'creative collaboration between the therapeutic impulse and the organizing principle and that, in the treatment of these most chaotic and anxious young people, neither element will get very far without the other' (p.203).

The necessity of supervision and consultancy

Simmonds (1988) says: 'What goes on inside people is not a comfortable subject of study for most organizational theorists and rarely a concern of management consultants or senior managers.' However, such a reluctance to explore this area denies the core task of an environment providing treatment. By offering a child an environment in which she is able to make emotionally secure relationships and recover from her trauma, the recovery team must act as containers for her emotional world. Instead of reacting to presenting behaviours the recovery team members are to withstand, reflect upon and eventually give meaning to these behaviours. The ability of the team to experience and contain the painful emotions projected on to them enables the child to take back the feelings again in a more manageable form. However, such a process can feel like an intrusive onslaught on the team's very sense of being and identity, which will inevitably stimulate their own primitive basic needs and unconscious defences. A danger may arise here that what the child projects on to the team becomes the trigger for the team to act out rather than be the source of understanding. Feelings that are painful to the children can also evoke extreme pain in the carers which they too may wish to defend against. Simmonds (1988) speaks of patients and analysts but what he says is also true of child and carer:

> in its raw state what the patient projects into the analyst becomes the source of acting out in the analyst rather than of understanding. Just as a feeling can be painful to the patient and evacuated, so it can evoke painful feelings in the analyst and be defended against.

In such circumstances the countertransference, which comprises all the feelings that the team experiences in relation to the child, is not properly used to understand the transference but causes inappropriate reactions due to the carers' own difficulties. Such potentially undesired feelings and responses can not only affect the carer's ability to help the child, but also the ability of the team as a whole to help the children.

The ability of the carers to engage in such therapeutic relationships with the children is dependent, therefore, not just on their knowledge of theory and understanding of the child and their personal capacity to explore, understand and contain their own emotional world, but critically on the organization having the structure and resources that will enable such exploration and understanding to occur in an effective and productive way.

It has been suggested that we often pursue a career which reflects a need within ourselves. In the caring or treatment professions such needs may be about a desire to help, save, control, take or give; or they may be about accepting the past or preparing for the future. Such motivations may well be unconscious and not feature in an individual's understanding of his intentions. However, when engaging in therapeutic relationships the carer is likely to be put in touch with these previously unconscious needs and feelings, some of which may cause him great distress and anxiety. The ability to contain these feelings is a greater task given the potential bombardment of feelings from the children. Copley and Forryan (1987) describe the dangers when they write that:

> not being good enough or not getting it right, feeling helpless, feeling intrusive, or, perhaps in reverse, feeling intruded upon, feeling lost and confused, are liable to beset most of us at times when attempting new endeavors or difficult situations. This is doubly difficult when we have to be relating to our own anxieties and distinguishing them from feelings evoked by the client. (p.40)

Very often supervision in child care, as in other types of agency, can revolve around management concerns. That is one kind of supervision and a necessary one, but it is not to be substituted for or confused with the supervision that allows staff to think about the children and their own feelings in relation to them. However, this does not imply that management itself is in some way divorced from this kind of supervision: such supervision has to be an integral part of effective and creative management. Wilson's (2003) point that the supervisor is 'the lynchpin' of an organization underlines this. The supervisor sits in the hierarchy responsible for those below him and responsible to those above him, but he is also providing part of the lifeblood of good practice and good management that courses through the veins of the organization. Preston-Shoot and Agass (1990) point out:

If social workers are to survive and be effective they require adequate preparatory training and good on-going supervision. Without it their exposure to anxiety, anger and the dependency feelings of clients, to emotional and physical overload, is likely to erode their intellectual and emotional resources, their morale and their confidence.

They [staff] are less likely to be able to retain their skills and strengths, or to develop their ability to practice competently. They are more likely to experience difficulties in keeping to their tasks and roles and retaining direction, and may succumb to collusive participation with service users: that is to form a closed system as a result of the emotional pressures and dynamics contained within the work. (p.162)

Supervision, they advise, is the way in which practitioners can monitor their interventions and effectiveness. It allows them to check 'whether they are seeing what they want to see and not seeing what they want to miss'. It allows them to analyse what is happening and to look critically at their decisions while tackling their own blind spots. Tomlinson (2004) refers to five aspects of what he calls 'the supervision of therapeutic work':

1. Ensuring that each team member is aware of therapeutic matters and understands the basic approach.

2. Creating the occasion when the concerns of the person supervised can be aired and explored.

3. Training which allows the supervisor to help the supervisee to underpin his practice with theory.

4. 'Managing in the sense of giving direction where necessary.'

5. 'Providing a reliable and protected space for supervision.' (pp.176–177)

Mirroring and countertransference reactions not only work from the children to carers but there is also the potential for the carers to affect the dynamics of the children's group (see Chapter 5) and the relationships between the two, as well as across to other relationships and groups.

Although the idea of mirroring might seem to be unhelpful in that it implies an unhealthy re-enactment or an enmeshment in a dynamic, if used reflectively it can serve as a valuable source of information to the team or individual. Careful examination and reflection on the team's presenting behaviours can tell us much about the current functioning and dynamic of the children's group. Such information can then be reflected upon in assessment meetings or team meetings and may direct the recovery plan for a child or the approach to the group as a whole through children's meetings and the therapeutic milieu of daily living.

It is essential, then, to recognize that one of the big problems for carers is that their unconscious investment in these children means there is a risk that a child may try to repeat her previous traumatic experiences and relationships. The carers take on the prescribed roles and teams or individuals can get caught up in the dynamic and become so enmeshed with the child that they will re-enact the child's previous history or relationships. This happens when carers are unable to step back and think objectively. They become stuck by taking up a role in the child's life and acting upon whatever a child is projecting on to them. The carer's emotions are so intense that they block his true perception and he seeks to meet the child's perceived needs, rather than her real ones.

Lucy: When the past is re-enacted

Nine-year-old Lucy had been abused by her father, who doted on her, but before the abuse took place she had to perform for him: she would dance, sing, or tell a story. When she was being therapeutically parented, she would also perform; for example, she would want to stage a play before bedtime. She would tell her therapist her story in the form of a drama. To the team this seemed to be a confirmation of her talents but, in fact, it was the re-enactment of her grooming by her father. This kept her at the centre of attention in the home and made her attractive. It was something with which the team colluded; indeed, it was something which attracted even non-practitioners, like receptionists, on the staff. However, she had to break from this by developing relationships that were not dependent on her having to be an entertainer with the expectation of abuse.

The highly intensive nature of therapeutic parenting within a residential setting gives potential for enmeshment to increase. As stated earlier, the child's own history may also reflect something in the carer's history so that, for example, he may re-enact his own parenting. Projection can create the role of victim or perpetrator and may bring with it feelings such as sadness, manic happiness or aggression.

Just as children's feelings need containing, so do those of adults who work with them. In doing this the supervisor's value is that he has a distance from the actual case and yet knows a child's history. He listens to how the team works and the relationships its members create, and is able to make links between history and the present. Supervision enables a carer to express his own feelings and think about them and respond to the child appropriately rather than reflecting the child's projection.

However, as we have said, powerful feelings from the children may not just impact on individuals but affect how the recovery team and indeed the organization functions as a whole. An example of this is that of a team which disliked a child even though objectively she was not dislikable. What they did was to re-enact her family background where she had been the scapegoat of her parents and her brothers and sisters had taken the lead from them.

The consultant is a step further removed from the supervisor because he comes from outside the organization. He is thus able to help the team make links between their sense of their own dynamic and the histories of the children. Consultants can offer the operational teams a resource that supports, encourages and improves their ability to help children to recover. This can be done by their establishing a forum to provide a reflective space within which individual and group themes and dynamics can be explored. Such a forum will aim at increasing understanding and linking feelings and anxieties into theory and practice.

Whitwell (1994), referring to therapeutic communities – but the same applies to staff working in the situation we describe – says that there is a danger of staleness setting in. New members who were not around in the early days find things established through routines, norms and expectations. How, then, he asks should good staff morale be maintained as the gloss wears off 'and the real grimness of the work begins to surface'? He talks about the need to 'keep the spirit of inquiry alive' and to do this, among the things needed are:

> External advisers – consultants – who can monitor, appraise and clinically supervise the work of the therapeutic community. They must not be seduced by the 'we' feeling. They must be a constant source of irritation in their quest to help the therapeutic community stay 'on task'. Residential units provide a rich breeding ground for bad practice being re-defined as good practice by this inward-looking 'we' group. Consultants need to see this and challenge it. (Whitwell 1994, pp.6–7)

What is described in this chapter is all part of creating that essential culture which Lanyado (1981) describes: 'An organizational structure which formally encourages us to learn to listen to each other more is ultimately not a luxury but a necessity and one which, I think, we are all ultimately thankful for' (p.146).

Exercises

1. If you are a carer for traumatized children, what support does your organization offer to help you in your role?

2. Does this support enable you to reflect upon your emotional world as well as the more practical tasks you undertake?

3. What other things do you do to help you cope with the demands of your role?

CHAPTER 5

A Place for Us
Creating a Therapeutic Environment

The physical environment

A home is more than a house, more than four walls. How we decorate and look after where we live, what is hung on the walls, the care with which furniture is bought and cared for, how ornaments and mementos of holidays are displayed – all these things are what turn a house into a home. A home will say much about who lives in it and how they regard it and themselves.

This is no less true for children living in residential care: the condition of the home – *their* home – says something to them about how they are regarded and what they are encouraged to make of it. It says something too about how they should regard their home. So our explanation of therapeutic parenting must address the fact that the physical environment in which children live can in many ways be as important as the emotional one and the relationships they share. The home in which a child in care lives will have as great a significance for her as the home of any child, but perhaps for different reasons. Traumatized children have often experienced a transitory and chaotic life. For some the residential home may be the first 'home' they have experienced and they may well have no real concept of what a 'home' means and could be like. This home will therefore be very important for their feelings of safety, rootedness and security.

In therapeutic parenting, the physical environment is specifically designed to meet the needs of the children. Matching the *total* mindfulness required of therapeutic parenting is the *total* environment in which it is practised. Underpinning this is the concept that *every* part of a child's life is seen as offering the potential for a therapeutic opportunity. Therefore, the home is structured, decorated and furnished in such a way that the everyday details reflect this.

Thus, it is not only how carers act towards a child that is important in challenging her inner working model; the physical environment can also do that. It can provide a feeling of belonging that assists her developing sense of identity and worth by reflecting her presence there. Take small but important examples of how this can be done: her picture is placed in the living room with those of the other children who live there; her school paintings and drawings can be stuck on the fridge; she can have her own place at the table, with her own napkin and mug.

A therapeutic physical environment, like a healthy home, should show every sign of being carefully thought about: colours, decoration and furniture. A child's room should be decorated and furnished to her own taste. This tells the child that she is worth the comfort, quality, thought and attention to detail. She comes to learn that it is also a thoughtful and safe environment where her needs are met. A home that is sufficiently situated within the local community tells the child that she doesn't have to be hidden away, but she is living in a place where privacy and safety are protected.

These children have been deprived of almost everything, physically and emotionally. Very often when they have been given anything it has been for an ulterior motive: it may have been a toy to allow the abuser to seek to reassure them or to seduce them into a false sense of security. Thus, it is important that the home should have a sense of plenty: games, art, ornaments, plants, furnishings, toys, comics and books. It should be child centred and reflect the personalities and needs of the children who live there. Small family-based homes for up to five children can give them the opportunity to develop relationships within a protected environment.

It is important to create a setting for children that is supportive, pleasant to live in and aesthetically pleasing. This is one way in which to tell the children how we feel about them. When they come to understand and internalize this, it will form the basis of how they feel about themselves. Surroundings that, in effect, say 'you are entitled to the best because you are an individual who is valued' will allow a child to come to know that this is the case. They are individuals whom others value, care for and protect. Everything is centred on them to meet their needs; it is stable, reliable and predictable.

A home where children live should reflect their personalities as much as those of their parents. Within a residential home this is even more important. The carers who work there may sleep in, but it is not their home; it is, however, home to the children.

Any good parents will know almost instinctively what kind of positive surroundings they will provide for their child. Even before a baby is born the parents think about how they will decorate and furnish the baby's room – the pretty curtains, the cot, the toys – creating a feeling of openness, light and security. Children who have been abused also deserve such thought and planning, but when they come into care (mostly) they are not babies; more often babies are taken into foster or adoptive care. For many children the experience of entering care will be of an institutionalized, impersonal, practical environment; one which shows little evidence of personal and individual investment. So planning a therapeutic environment for these children requires much thought and attention to detail in every aspect because of what is trying to be communicated to them and how, given their internal working model, they will experience it.

What can this mean in practice? A home must offer a sense of warmth and comfort. This is more easily achieved, for example, if floors are not left bare and rugs and mats are used. Thought should be given to the materials of which things are made and what these may symbolically represent; for example, a wooden door may represent solidity, what is natural and wholesomeness; a glazed door allows people to see in but also those within to be seen. Doors can let people in as well as keep them out. Thus, like windows, they can represent different things to different children. For some they may offer security, a barrier to keep away threats from outside; for others windows may allow what is outside to be seen and enjoyed. Children who have been abused often have no sense of boundary; it has been trampled on, where it ever existed, by emotional and physical onslaught. They have lived in frequently chaotic homes constantly invaded by strangers, who will often have abused them, who will have come and gone without warning, leaving the child not knowing what to expect.

It is helpful for doors to be secured and generally shut, thereby necessitating someone actually having to allow a visitor to enter rather than the door being open and visitors free to enter at will. The house should be one where children know who is visiting, who is in at any one time and so should not be surprised or made anxious by unknown intruders.

It is helpful for all windows to have curtains. Again attention to the quality and material will be needed to ensure they allow the light through but keep the warmth in. The addition of an inner curtain such as nets or muslin would ensure large expanses of glass are kept feeling contained with the inside and outside not unhelpfully exposed during the daytime.

Thought should be given to the colours with which rooms are decorated because colours can influence mood. It is important not to try to impose an emotional state upon a child by the choice of colour; choosing neutral colours can help avoid this. Carers should try to be aware of the possible links a child may have with some colours and think about why a child chooses a certain colour for their bedroom. It may be appropriate for a child to be encouraged to select again or to limit the choices available. Lighting creates atmosphere; dimmer switches, nightlights and lamps can help set the scene for bedtime as well as offer security for children at night.

The outside of a home is as important as the inside. The children we refer to will rarely have known safety or consistent boundaries. Attention to the outside of a property can help create a sense of this for the child. Homes should ideally have a physical boundary that separates it from neighbouring structures. This may perhaps take the form of a fence or hedge. As with boundaries in relationships, physical boundaries should be well maintained and respected. A hole in the fence or dead hedge may feel less containing for such children; they may feel they could fall out or that danger could get in. Symbolically, they may think that this suggests that their carers will not contain them and keep them safe from what may unhelpfully impinge on them.

Like the inside of the home, gardens should be well maintained and cared for. Grass needs to be cut regularly, hedges trimmed and a colourful selection of plants and shrubs planted to reflect the seasons of the year, as well as symbolizing our ability to grow and keep things alive. This symbolic representation of the process of nurture and growth can be of great benefit to children in their recovery. Garden furnishings provide a further opportunity for the carers to reflect the needs of the children within the home and careful selection of activity equipment can offer opportunities for play and relaxation.

It is fundamentally important that the children gain a real sense that within the home there is space for everyone, particularly that they feel there is a protected space for them. Careful forward planning on details such as enough seats being laid at the dining table is vital to assure a child that she is held in mind, has a place and is wanted. Turning up to lunch and there being no place would raise emotions in even the most confident among us.

If children feel they can leave some of their belongings – say, a toy or game – around the home, they are more likely to feel ownership and a sense of belonging to the community of the home. They begin to feel that the whole home is somewhere to which they can bring themselves rather than feeling that part of them is tucked away in a bedroom.

As we have said, where these children have lived in the past may well be neglected, chaotic and uncared for and they may have come to believe that this is what they are worthy of. They were familiar with it and it was an environment where they managed to survive. Ironically, they may also feel that in many ways it was a safe environment for them. Thus, in the same way that traumatized children may re-create a negative but familiar relationship with their carers, they may also try to re-create their previous physical chaos in their new environment and attempt to damage or disrupt the home. How staff understand this and what they do about it will symbolize their ability to withstand the emotional damage of the children and the staff's wish to help make things better, to heal and mend. All damage within the home should, therefore, be repaired or replaced as soon as possible.

Children should not feel that they are being punished for their neglect or the damage they cause. Rather, they should be given to understand that their carers see this as a communication to be understood and given meaning. However, this can be easier said than done. It is no easy thing for carers to retain their understanding of why some children act negatively and attack the very home which the carers try to look after – and this can often happen day in and day out for lengthy periods. It is perhaps understandable for them to see what is happening as an attack on their hard work and creativity, yet they are required to continue to care for the child and be motivated to repair, replace and invest. This is an achievement that perhaps can only be sustained if the carers really do understand and believe in the symbolic nature of the task and have the opportunity to process and express the emotions evoked in them through such behaviours. At times, the carers may feel exasperated when a child is negative or destructive, perhaps causing havoc with something the carer has worked on in the house for several days.

However understandable this may be, carers should try not to react impulsively in an angry or uncontrolled way but attempt to respond. They must never display their visceral feelings but try to be reflective and thoughtful towards what a child has done. Team meetings, supervision and consultations are clearly important and necessary opportunities where carers have the chance to express and share the feelings they are struggling to contain.

Children who have been neglected often have no real experience of being looked after by others. They have little or no belief that others could look after them or the ability to appropriately look after themselves. It can often be difficult at first for such children to allow a carer to offer individualized nurture and care and, therefore, difficult for the carer to challenge the child's belief that this is possible. However, through the carer demonstrating his ability and determination to consistently look after the environment in which the child lives, he is able to display symbolically his desire and commitment to looking after the child.

Thus, it would be inappropriate to expect these children to look after their home. The therapeutic parenting team is able to indicate to the child that they recognize and understand this and show that they are able to look after the child. They can demonstrate this by being willing to look after the home. It is important that carers do this obviously and actively by cleaning and tidying routines. They should be prepared to be the ones left to make good at the end of the day and be seen to be doing so.

Just as it would be unreasonable to expect a child to have trust in others to look after her, so it would be entirely inappropriate to expect her to look after others and their environment. We would not expect an infant to undertake such tasks as they would not be developmentally able – a direct parallel with the older child who is also not developmentally able. It may well be appropriate to have higher expectations for children approaching recovery who may be ready to do more to help in this way. The decisions about this would be explored as part of the child's recovery assessment and would form part of their individual recovery plan (see Chapter 10).

The skill in meeting these challenges (as with others) depends on how children are communicated with and being attuned to what they are trying to let their carers know. All behaviour – a child damaging the home, even a child hitting another – should be seen as a form of communication that needs to be understood.

A child's bedroom is an important and symbolic space for her, not least because a bedroom may be redolent of memories of some of the worst things that have happened to her. It is sometimes argued that a child's bedroom should not be interfered with by the carers, even if this means the space is unkempt and chaotic. The reason, the argument goes, is that this is the child's space and any interference with it is to intrude upon her privacy. However, what we have said so far about the physical environment applies to bedrooms no less than anywhere else. Children need to be helped to live within a healthy, valuing and nurturing environment, even if this means that for some children this is fully created and maintained for them by the therapeutic parenting team. The bedroom which is allotted to a child when she comes into the home is her own. It is a space in the house which people seek her permission to enter. Even before she moves in it begins to take on her personality and preferences.

The daily routine

As we have outlined, traumatized children have often lacked a sense of routine in their lives. Routine can create a sense of reliability, consistency and predictability, which in turn can create a sense of safety and containment. Therefore, the provision of a well-planned and reliable daily routine in a home creates the opportunity to offer a containing and therapeutic environment for the children. Although each child will have her own individual recovery plan, this is carried out within the context of a daily communal routine.

Johnny: The importance of structure and routines

Johnny's mother had a personality disorder and his father was assessed as having psychopathic traits. They had met when patients in a psychiatric hospital. She had had five children with different men, most of whom were violent with drugs and alcohol problems.

Johnny was placed on the child protection register at birth for neglect and emotional harm. When a young child his mother would repeatedly abandon him and his brothers and sisters for long periods of time, leaving him feeling uncertain and deserted. He witnessed fighting and sexual violence and was himself physically abused. Perhaps to comfort themselves, the children indulged in sexual acts.

Johnny was brought into care at the age of eight. He had experienced numerous short-term foster placements and several quite inappropriate residential placements before being referred to a therapeutic placement. Most placements had found his aggressive, sexualized behaviour very difficult. In one foster placement he waited until he was alone with the foster mother and then demanded sex from her, grabbing her inner thighs and thrusting forwards with an erection in evidence.

In this latest placement he tried to create the chaos he had experienced and was feeling by displaying very challenging, aggressive and sexualized behaviour. Johnny found the positive reinforcement of consistent, safe boundaries difficult. He tried in every way to disrupt the routines and milieu of the house. Understanding his inner turmoil meant that a plan for containment could be devised to be followed by all carers. Every area of his life was systematically assessed. What was his behaviour? Why did we think he was doing something? What would his carers' response be and why this particular response? This enabled those working with him to understand him better and how they responded to his behaviour, and make a plan which could be maintained. The plan for Johnny was based on the idea that if nurturing is positively reinforced, in time it will allow the child to develop their own internal controls and choices in a healthy way.

Thus, when it came to going to bed Johnny was told that the time for bed would be in ten minutes. He would be accompanied, not sent alone to his bedroom, his room having been prepared for him with, for example, the lamp turned on, the bed turned back and curtains closed. He would be read a story and tucked in, ensuring he knew who would be around during the night.

The carers would make sure they were being consistent by following the plan and doing what they said they would do. They would also inform other carers in the therapeutic parenting team of their actions which promoted a sense of openness and honesty to encourage trust to develop.

The day ends...

What happens when a child goes to bed can go a long way towards helping her when she wakes the next morning. There is much preparation for morning which could be undertaken after children have settled in their beds. Fulfilling the practical tasks of parenting and housekeeping the night before may allow the therapeutic parenting team time to prepare themselves to be emotionally, as well as physically, available to the children in the morning.

Clearing up the home at the end of the day helps not only to provide a containing and nurturing environment, but can also symbolically contain the child's emotional disturbance. This is particularly the case if a child has become distressed and has communicated this through displays of behaviour which have left the home marked or damaged in some way. If both the child and the home can be 'resettled' that night it will more likely allow the day to be ended and a new day begun the next. Drawing a conclusion and making reparation can reduce the potential for the child to feel shame and guilt about the damage; feelings which may be unbearable for a child and trigger similar acting out again. For carers too, such end of the day activity allows them to put whatever has occurred behind them, along with any feelings that may affect the way they interact with the children.

The very act of preparing bed, tidying and thinking about the next day and what to wake for is in itself a contrast to the chaotic lives that the children will have lived. They can see from what is being done by way of preparation that this is something thought about because of how it affects them and what is best for them.

There are many tasks for the carers to do and the children to learn from: the house needs tidying, clearing and cleaning, and bedrooms need warming and getting ready. There is a need to ensure that any individual provision is ready. Each child has special towels and toiletries; her school uniform is clean and ironed; shoes are polished; lunch prepared and packed; and schoolbags ready, with books and homework complete. Breakfast for the next day needs preparing with cereals and so on laid on the table. Places are laid out and fully equipped and kettles are filled, and so on.

Thought can also be given to the day that has passed, as well as checking the diary for the day ahead and ensuring that appointments will be kept, with everyone knowing who is to do what and when. Carers must allow time for themselves so that they can sleep easily and be prepared emotionally for the next day. All of this allows carers to deal with anything unexpected the following morning without it impinging on the children's routines. These routines also allow a sense of team work among carers, which itself contributes to what they can offer the children.

Children need to be told who is sleeping in, who will wake them and who will undertake the morning routines with them. When children see carers going about their tasks, they come to understand not only that this is being done for them but in time it may allow them too to take on some of the tasks. When they invest in where they live, they may start to invest in themselves.

Going to bed may be a particularly anxious time for a child who has been abused. Children who have had positive early experiences and are free from trauma may feel secure in bed; the warmth and comfort and the prospect of soothing dreams and carefree sleep. But for a child who has been abused even a bed may be something about which she is ambivalent because of what may have happened to her in bed. She may well be more likely to suffer nightmares and night terrors rather than dreams.

Some children will not sleep because they fear someone coming into the room. Some children will sleep under the bed or with layers of bedclothes on them in order to protect themselves. Other children may not seek to protect themselves in this way but attempt to re-create past situations and so perhaps to test out their safety by going to bed naked.

Bedtime is also a time of letting go, of knowing that a state of unconsciousness awaits, but also that while we are asleep others may be up and about. What prospect might that offer to a child who is being asked to willingly give way to unconsciousness? During the day a child will find points of reference, people who offer security and safety, or objects of comfort and refuge. But during the night they may not be available. Going to sleep perhaps requires more trust on the part of the abused child than we tend to imagine so carers need to think about how to support the child.

Daws (1993) points out that 'the interchange between parents and baby about going to bed and getting to sleep is, like feeding, one of the crucial transactions between them' (p.2). She goes on to say:

> Sleeping problems illustrate difficulties at every stage. Receptivity to the needs of a baby, sensitivity to their fears and spontaneous offering of comfort need to be tempered with a gradual setting of limits. Understanding of a baby's fears enables a parent to contain those fears; the baby gradually learns to manage them himself. (p.4)

If a child starts to show anxiety near bedtime, carers can try to counteract this through individual provision as agreed in the individual recovery plan; perhaps offering a story, hot milk, the comfort blanket, the cuddly toy who is her symbolic companion, the pleasures of bathtime.

As bedtime approaches, it is not helpful for children to be encouraged to engage in activities that spark excitement or tension. Perhaps earlier in the evening they will have played games that use up energy (and thus entice sleepiness) but now is the time for toys, reading, board games, and the like. Many children like to have a nightlight or lights which gradually dim. Bedtime for everyone is a time for quiet, so noise especially needs to be kept to a minimum.

...and the day begins

Getting out of bed the right or wrong side, as the saying goes, is something that affects us all. How we start the day very often influences how the rest of the day will be for us and others. But how children who have been abused wake – who wakes them, what they see and hear when they awake – can resonate deeply with their trauma. Attention here may therefore play a significant part in their recovery process. Going a step back, preparing for them to wake is crucial to the daily routines and structure of a house. How that takes place can very much affect the day for both the child and the carer.

What we do to prepare children for their waking can allow them to experience actually and symbolically the emotional investment which we are making in them. As Brown (undated) reminds us: 'Waking up can be a particularly difficult and painful process for emotionally disturbed children because their past experiences have not led them to expect anything good to come from the coming day' (p.1).

Wherever possible a child should be woken by someone with whom they have a significant relationship. This is another way in which a child develops her relationship with a carer, especially the key carer if he is available. Practical considerations will mean that this is not always possible, but it is important that when this cannot be so the child is not awoken by agency staff or staff members new to the house. It is very obvious that a child seeing someone unknown to her may bring back memories of her own abuse by strangers coming in and out of her family home.

It is also important that children be fully involved in establishing waking up routines, which should be part of their individual recovery plans and reviewed as necessary. The plan should be as detailed as possible, outlining anything provided for a particular child (for example, whether she likes to be woken and given a glass of milk), any agreed physical contact, and what both child and carer expect at the time of waking. The child should be involved with what will happen, what time the carer will come into the room and be told the night before who that will be.

Touch can be significant in a child's waking up and again this is something with which the child should be involved in discussing. Likewise, a carer should not sit on a child's bed because it is the only option but because a child finds it helpful or reassuring. Thus, a chair should always be part of the furniture in a child's room.

It is important that we do not assume how a child would wish to be woken. A loud, bright voice and the curtains suddenly pulled back with the sun beaming into the room may suit some children but not others. What happens when a child is awake? What does she see and experience as she leaves her bedroom? A welcoming house is one which will be warm, curtains drawn or open as needs be, towels are warming, and the smell of hot toast and drinks coming from the kitchen. A radio may be on, but thought should be given to the volume and type of music played.

Children who are further on in their recovery will be able to do more for themselves at this time. They may be able to wash and dress themselves, prepare their own breakfast and do jobs around the house.

Bathing and personal hygiene

Our discussion of play fighting and tickling (see p.69) shows that replicating a healthy development and parenting through therapeutic parenting can sometimes only be approximate to the real thing. This is the case with some other aspects of the ordinary life of children who have been abused, perhaps most obviously with bathing and personal hygiene.

Most children develop a more or less healthy understanding of their body and its functions as they grow up, and can be helped by the mature and healthy attitudes of their parents. Children frequently go through phases about their bodies and how they work: for example, small children's interest in faeces or little boys' and girls' amusement with penises. Healthy children explore their bodies on their own or with other children in the games they play.

All of this may be vastly different for the abused child. She may hardly have had time to discover much about her body before it had been violated by an adult. She may be left with a sense that her body is something desired by adults who hurt her as they realize that desire, which in turn can leave her with a sense of guilt and self-loathing, hatred even of her own body. Neither does the disrespect for her body end with the way it is used sexually. Abused children may also have been neglected in their feeding, hygiene and primary nurture. Often there will have been little or nothing to tell them that adults value children's bodies as something to be cared for, nurtured and protected. Their bodies are often the vessels of the negative memories and experiences they carry, a constant reminder not only of what has happened to them but of how little they are worth.

Thus, anyone who is responsible for a child's physical care has to bear in mind the biography which the child brings with her and what her body may represent to her. Here then is another practical matter where a child's physical care also provides an opportunity to meet, actually and symbolically, earlier unmet emotional needs. Bathing offers a good example of this because how it happens relies on a child's chronological and developmental needs. Consider what needs are met by bathing a child: the development and continuation of an attachment; physical nurture; offering care and concern; opportunities for role modelling; education; soothing; playing; establishing a routine; doing something with the child; and physical touch.

Claire: Making bathtime a pleasure

Quite early on in her life, Claire was neglected, abused and conditioned by parents who were both quite strongly within a satanic culture. She was locked in a cellar without food for extended periods. She was made to wash her face and hair in the blood of animals, and she was held under water with the threat of death if she did not comply or if she spoke out. She was conditioned to go to the toilet prior to the abuse occurring. This abuse could be with several people during an evening. The process of being bathed was a precursor for abuse. For Claire the healthy enjoyable pastime of being bathed and being clean had sinister repercussions. When she was not being abused she would not need to wash or bathe.

When she was ten Claire was placed in a therapeutic environment. She was unkempt and dirty and looked uncared for – a waif and stray. She became anxious and aggressive at bathtime, especially in the evenings. She refused to allow a carer into the bathroom but would not wash her face or hair.

To help her overcome these barriers her carer spoke to her about why it was good to be bathed, about washing her hair and face. She was given a clear message about the routine, which she helped to create – that her bath would be run at a certain time, what things she wanted in the bath would be provided, with lots of toys, bubble bath of her choosing if she wished. She also liked sponges and flannels of her favourite play items. The carer would be outside the bathroom initially, reassuring her that she was safe and asking if she wanted her back or hair washed.

The carer would see that her towels, which were big, soft and colourful, were ready and warm. Her bathrobe, slippers, clothes or pyjamas were also made ready. She was reassured before and after that she was safe and would not be harmed. She was shown and told how to dry herself and to have creams applied to her body.

As the relationship developed and her sense of safety increased and Claire became aware that other children were being cared for and enjoyed being bathed, she allowed the carer to bath her. These actions were carried out sympathetically and at her pace to allay Claire's fears. To ensure water or soap did not go into her eyes she had swimming goggles both as playthings and for protection. Later she was encouraged to wash herself in an orderly manner from her head downwards and told the reasons for this.

She was given lots of praise following each step. She was told how well she looked all 'clean and shiny'. As this routine continued, many of her fears associated with being bathed dissolved and she became able to enjoy what for most of us is a pleasurable experience.

Small children enjoy being bathed. Water running, splashing around in the bath, playing with the soapsuds, having plastic ducks and other toys floating about them, getting out of the water into a warm towel and the parent's embrace and a quick rub down and playfulness – these are memories of the everydayness of a happy childhood shared by many people.

But what if the child behaves younger than her chronological years? She cannot be treated as if she were that young age. It would not be appropriate for the therapeutic parenting team to treat, say, a 13-year-old in the same way as a 3- or 4-year-old. How then to re-create appropriately that babying experience which the child will have missed? Water can be run, lotions made available, sweet-smelling soap put into the bath, and warm towels laid out and prepared for later. This allows something of the actual missed experience as well as having symbolic value. Preparing the bath, respect for her individual preferences (that colour soap or this colour soap), bubble bath, temperature, favourite toy in the bath, flannel, shampoo, the time of the day – these provide a child with the sense of being held in mind, cared for and nurtured.

It may not be always appropriate for a carer to be in the bathroom at all times but he can still show his care for the child in other ways. For some children, a bathroom may be a place that is fearful and lonely. Thus, the sound of the carer's voice through the door may be soothing, while for other children, the sound of carers tidying on the landing may be helpful.

No matter how old the child, some actual physical care can be given, like helping her to wash her hair, hands, face and teeth. These give the child an actual experience of physical contact and care. Not everything will suit all children and each child must be considered individually. What the child wants will often be given in the clues she provides as her relationship with the carer develops. Meeting children's individual needs in physical care can be done in a very practical way. Each child should have her own set of toiletries, which she may have helped to choose at a visit to the local chemist or supermarket. These will be kept either in her bedroom or by the carers. Each child should also have her own flannel and set of towels in a colour of her choice.

While some children will have razors and aerosols (provided after a risk assessment), these may need to be looked after securely by carers because of the other children. But if this is the case, then it is important that safety measures be explained to the children so they cannot infer any shortcoming on their part.

Practising good hygiene should be encouraged at all times: it is part of the instilling of self-respect as well as respect for others. Children should have to wash their hands before preparing and eating food, just as they should after visiting the bathroom. Carers being seen to replace the toilet roll, clean the toilet, rinse the sink, and so on demonstrate not just the importance of personal hygiene but also an acceptance and appreciation of our normal bodily functions. Openness about the body, its functions and cleanliness should always bear in mind a child's previous experience.

It is a good idea for children to be encouraged to change into slippers when coming into the house as this encourages respect for the home – that is, no walking with wet and muddy feet across carpets that someone else has

cleaned. But this also has a symbolic value in that it represents the importance of warmth. Having a pair of slippers allows another chance for a child
to have something of her own, which she can choose herself, to value and
care for.

When playing is more than a game

Several times in this book we have drawn attention to the fact that while
therapeutic parenting is giving a child the care and attention which she has
been denied and by so doing rebuild her ability to make attachments, there
are nevertheless some areas where we have to tread cautiously in a
way which would not necessarily occur with other children. We have
mentioned with bedtime and bathing how the carer needs to be mindful of
the child's emotional age and also what would and would not be appropriate with a child who has been abused.

Other good examples of this are tickling and play fighting.[8] Whereas
these are very common games between children and adults, those working
with traumatized children need to give serious thought to whether to
indulge in what is otherwise harmless fun. Such intimate physical activity
may be misunderstood by children who may have been physically and
sexually abused, giving rise to complicated and confusing feelings.

Anyone who has been tickled or who has tickled someone else knows
that the main feeling raised by it is that the person being tickled feels completely out of control; they are, literally, at the mercy of the tickler as to
when it will end. They are helpless at the hands of another. It is not difficult
to see that for a child who has been abused this experience may too easily
echo the many negative experiences she has already undergone. Play
fighting and tickling invade their personal space and also militate against
the attempt of therapeutic parenting to help a child establish the idea that
they own their bodies; it is their decision how they make use of them or
give consent to how others may or may not touch them.

Because tickling and play fighting are aggressive – the impulsive
reaction is 'When I get the upper hand I will do this to you' or 'If I escape
from this tickling, just wait until I can tickle you' – they can stir up sexual
and aggressive feelings. They can let loose feelings and emotions in a
situation where the carer strives for them to be contained.

Tickling and play fighting are fun for most children. The 'hurt' that a child feels when that sort of play takes place is all part of the fun. She enjoys it, just as she enjoys being 'scared'. It passes away (insofar as it can ever be regarded meaningfully as hurt or real terror) and the child rests secure in the knowledge that the adult with whom she has fought or who has tickled her is someone who loves her, cares for her and protects her. She knows this not only by the spirit in which the experience takes place but the experience she has of the adult generally. However, Tomlinson (2004) says:

> As tickling and play fighting are meant to be 'just fun', it can be hard to acknowledge any difficulties which arise. These feelings might then come out somewhere else. Tickling and play fighting can be confusing to a child who has been hurt physically or emotionally by someone who also loved him. The distinction between being cared for and being hurt is blurred. (p.207)

He goes on to say that there should be a 'clear message' that care and hurt do not go together and points to other blurred distinctions: the line between play and fighting; who can do what to whom – adult to child, child to adult – and is there any difference when one is male and one is female?

Children who have been traumatized are still children who want what all children want, which includes play and fun, so if a child attempts to start tickling or attempts play fighting, she shouldn't be left feeling rejected when the carer discourages it. It might be difficult for the child to know how to make contact. But also while that child may well 'just want to play', she may also be testing the carer – if she acts in a certain way will he become involved and act inappropriately? Tomlinson (2004) makes a telling point when he states:

> It is helpful to be open to different physical approaches from a child, as it tells us something significant about him, but not necessarily to join in with it. At times, it will be necessary to say 'no' clearly to him. By making our own boundaries clear, we will also help him begin to get a sense of his own. (p.207)

Pets and animals

Many children love animals. A dog, cat or hamster – or sometimes all three! – can be treasured members of the family. Children take pleasure in animals because of their lovability and affection, and through caring for them and being concerned about them their area of sympathy or empathy is increased. The death of an animal can be keenly felt by a child. It may often be their first experience of death and a pet's death is a way in which some parents introduce children to the idea that life is finite and that we mourn those we love who die.

However, for many children who have been abused, pets like other things which for most children are a simple enjoyment or pleasure, can be problematic. Some children will have been hurt by animals or pets and some have witnessed or been party to their being abused. Animals may have been a part, direct or indirect, of their traumatic experiences and they associate them not with love, warmth and pleasure but terror, hurt, rage and guilt.

But there is also a very practical consideration about children who have been severely abused. They have little sense of their own needs, even less of an idea as to how to meet them and certainly no real sense of the needs of others. They are often delayed emotionally and developmentally, with little concept of guilt and empathy. They will often act and feel in a way much younger than their chronological age. It is not realistic to expect these children to be able to look after pets.

Most children are unable to look after a pet at a young age, and even a pet in the house may cause problems. Small children are quite capable of being cruel to animals without meaning to just because they have no idea how to deal with them. Being able to look after a pet requires a degree of maturity and sophistication. When pets are part of a family where there is a small child, it is usually the parents who end up looking after it, not the child. It is unreasonable to expect this of a therapeutic parenting team when they should be concentrating fully on the needs of the children.

Children who have been abused may also attempt to repeat or re-enact their traumatic experiences or relationships; some may have harmed animals, and might seek to harm any pet kept in the home. The impact this would have on both the child and others in the home may be great. The arousal of emotions caused by this can be so overwhelming and difficult to deal with that it can cause a placement to break down.

It can be argued that a relationship between a pet and a traumatized child can be positive and allows the child to learn to nurture and relate to another. This may be the case with some children in need of care but, whatever the benefits might be thought to be, the risk of something very negative and thus further damaging to a child is too great. This said, children do not have to be deprived of all contact with animals. They can have that experience at a safe distance which also allows enjoyment through visits to the zoo or to parks.

Group meetings

Societies are more than individuals; they are groups of individuals coming together for a shared purpose from sport to politics, from book reading to gardening, from an ad hoc campaign to an organization in existence for many years. When we meet in this way we come together with an objective to be achieved, views to air or a problem to be overcome. Human beings are social animals and thus the meeting is an expression of our oneness as a group that can do things together.

However, many children who have been severely abused have no sense of the group, and are unable to function as part of a group. This is because their experience of a group – notably their family – is one of breakdown and often fragmentation; it is certainly not one of caring for each other. Even when children have been associated with other kinds of group, the experience may have been the same: the foster home placement which broke down, the children's home where there was no security, or the school from which they were excluded.

Some children have yet to develop to the point where they have a sense of their own identity, as opposed to being an extension of someone else's. This means that their powers to empathize and understand what impact they have on others and around them is limited, if at times non-existent. Often the strongest sense they have is that of their own powerlessness.

Progress in recovery brings with it a sense of self, which in turn means that the child has to learn to empathize with others. To do this she needs to be encouraged to see beyond the primary relationship between herself and another to being part of a larger entity, the group. She sees this most obviously when members of a home are physically present together, which happens as part of daily life: mealtimes, video nights, and so on. However, times such as these may not actively engage the child as part of the group, or actively promote communication between her and the life of her home and her relationships with those with whom she lives. It is important, therefore, that there are specific times for this kind of coming together which is an active part of the child's recovery.

The children's meeting is such an opportunity. It allows children to see themselves as belonging to a group and sharing a common experience with others that can help take away the extreme isolation which many of them have. It gives them the chance to be listened to, and to feel that what they have to say is valued. A child can offer an opinion or make a choice; she can be a positive influence on the life of the home; and she can develop social and communication skills. A positive group experience (of course, there can be negative ones) is one where the child can see others supporting her and she, in turn, can learn to recognize their needs.

Gilly: Can you hear me?

Gilly's family background was one of violence, neglect and abuse. There were few boundaries and ineffectual parenting. Aggression, shouting, brawling and other antisocial methods had been the ways of communicating. She had little sense of how to speak to be heard and so either shouted or screamed louder and longer or became aggressive. The idea of speaking to others calmly about her thoughts and feelings was quite incomprehensible, anxiety provoking and pointless. Who wanted to listen to her anyway?

Her carer, by being like a calm, respectful and caring parent, demonstrated to her how she could share her feelings. He would explain the purpose of the meetings each time before they took place. He would check what issues she might have or wish to speak about. He would remind her that one was expected not to shout but to listen and talk quietly. He would ensure he sat close to her in the meetings and held her hand to reassure her, giving a gentle squeeze at times both to offer support and encouragement to speak.

He would praise her efforts and provide the containment for her anxieties and promote a positive way of relating to others. If things did not go well he would spend time following the meeting to talk about how it went, what was good and what could be better and how she felt. If her anxieties became too great, he would offer her the opportunity to have some time away from the group with the aim to go back into the meeting as soon as she was able.

Gilly was encouraged to speak and not shout, to listen to others, to be patient, to ask suitable questions and discuss things that were important to her. These were recorded and responded to, thus reinforcing that her thoughts, feelings and ideas were important and that she had a voice and was worthy of being heard.

Over time, being encouraged and supported to attend the group meetings, Gilly was enabled to speak about her achievements, feelings, thoughts and anxieties calmly and appropriately. She was later able to take this experience with her after leaving care and use it effectively in her work environment where she was required to meet daily to discuss the day's events.

While these meetings have a therapeutic value, they are also a practical necessity. They can be the forum where plans, events and changes to the home are announced or consulted about, and future projects planned. They are occasions where members can reflect on what has happened to them together, whether negative or positive. Relationships between members can be explored. Members can think about and affirm what is acceptable behaviour and the reasons for this, as well as talking about their feelings and the themes and dynamics of the meetings and, indeed, of the home.

The children's meeting is also of value to the therapeutic parenting team because it allows them to observe the dynamics and relationships within the home; the development of the children individually and as a group; and gives them a chance to act as role models in relationships, in the way that problems are solved and how we communicate and appropriately express feelings and emotions.

However, none of this is achieved easily and a meeting that works can be one where a lot of energy has been expended. Such meetings can also create anxiety which can easily be uncontained and thus cause problems. How this can be avoided is by thinking about the venue, the seating, the structure and the content of the meeting.

The meeting will very probably need to be held in the lounge or dining area if there is to be enough space for everyone to be comfortably accommodated. Seating should allow everyone to see one another. While this might well mean sitting in a circle, a circle does have an empty space in the middle with no boundary, symbolic or real, preventing that space being crossed. Some children can feel that this is unsafe. They may perceive that danger could cross the space and harm them. In which case, a coffee table or similar kind of furniture could be placed in the middle. Because abused children often have little sense of their own boundaries and rely on carers to create these for them, they could easily lose themselves in a meeting by merging with other children. Thus, it is helpful for staff to position themselves so that no two children sit next to each other or each child sits with her key or supporting carer.

Many meetings, no less a group meeting for traumatized children, have the potential to provoke anxiety so it is important that everything be done to promote calm and safety. Lighting can be important here and consideration should be given to using lamps or dimmer switches rather than very bright lights. The room should be comfortably warm and not oppressive and stuffy as this can cause sleepiness or fidgeting. If the meeting is held at dusk the curtains could be drawn beforehand to prevent the group finding themselves surrounded by the darkness outside. When the meeting is taking place the door should be closed so that the room is contained; this keeps members safely in and intrusion out.

The structure and boundaries of the children's meetings need to be clear and robust, reliable and consistent. While children can undermine the meeting, so too can anxiety arising from within the therapeutic parenting team, which means that it is important at meetings to observe structures. It is also important to explore any undermining of the meeting within supervision and in one-to-one meetings with the children.

Children's group meetings should take place at a minimum twice a week, ideally perhaps even more frequently, and last at most an hour and minimum half an hour. All children should attend along with all carers looking after the children at the time when the meeting takes place. (The house manager or his deputy should also be present.) A member of the therapeutic parenting team should chair the meeting. Meetings need to be held at a time when consistency and reliability can best be achieved. The timing should allow for preparation and for any necessary follow-up with individuals afterwards. The meetings should not impinge on other important therapeutic experiences; for example, they should not interfere with bedtimes and mealtimes. Minutes should be taken by one of the carers and not a child, and it should be clearly stated who is responsible for agreed actions and when they will be carried out.

We began by saying that how a home is looked after and decorated, the care with which its furniture and ornaments are chosen, and the way children are treated, with regard to their personal care, clothing and the consideration that goes towards making their room their own – these things tell the child much about how she is regarded and valued by her carers. This is true for all children, but in taking such steps with children who have been traumatized through abuse carers are creating an environment that is, by its nature, a healing one.

Exercises

1. Think about your home or place of work.

2. Imagine you are entering the space for the first time: what messages does the environment convey to you?

3. What messages would you like it to convey?

4. How could this change be achieved?

5. Reflect upon your average day from getting up to going to sleep.

6. What things do you do every day?

7. Are there certain rituals you have adopted?

8. Why do you think this is?

9. What if you stopped doing these things?

10. If you are a parent what routines did you develop for your children? Why did this seem important?

CHAPTER 6

The New Arrival
The Process of Admission

When a baby is expected, parents prepare for the birth in many different ways. Attachment theory calls this the 'claiming process', the beginning of Winnicott's 'maternal preoccupation' and of the child's primary attachment. The child can be seen to be 'claimed' by the parents in many ways: a name is chosen; a place in their home is created for her; clothes and provisions are bought; toys are chosen; announcements and celebrations take place. Thus, when a child is born she is provided for emotionally and physically. She is introduced to the wider family and in some cultures there are rituals of introduction (as well having a religious significance) like baptism. For a child who is being introduced to therapeutic parenting, her 'rebirth' – a 'claiming' – is seen as integral to her admission.

There are two important things to remember about a child's admission into residential care. First, it affects not only her but everyone else as well – staff and other children. Second, it is more than an administrative matter: it is the therapeutic beginning of a child's recovery, so how it is done is very important.

A new start or a new beginning may sound like a cliché but admission can be part of that very process, quite literally, for children who have been abused. They will not have experienced a positive beginning to their lives; rather than being 'claimed' they are likely to have been rejected. They will not have known good parenting through which a healthy attachment is made to those who care for them. Indeed, what they have known will probably have been a relationship which is responsible for their trauma.

Thus, therapeutic parenting offers the chance to begin again, a 're-parenting' with an attachment to parental figures which are symbolically akin to that of a baby and her mother.

The child's coming to her new home can therefore be seen to represent symbolically the child's birth into a family. The actual process and practicalities of a child's admission therefore warrant much thought and attention. This can be the opportunity for the child's 'birth' to offer her the foundations for her healthy emotional and physical development.

An admission plan is drawn up and shared with the recovery team. An outline of the admission process is also shared with the children and opportunities are given for their involvement. The admission plan has a number of elements, which are set out below. However, throughout this process the most important aspects are communication and the working together of the internal recovery team as a whole and the external agencies involved in placing the child. Without all parties working together the child is likely to fall through the gap and her move to her new home will be a time of anxiety and fear which will only serve to compound her already traumatized place in the world.

Initial visit to the child by the key carer and home manager

This introduces the child to the agency and her future carers. It is undertaken in an environment familiar to the child, which may be the residential or foster home or secure unit where she presently lives, and will help prepare for her visit to her new home. Just as a firstborn child awaits the arrival of a brother or sister, the involvement in the new child's arrival at the home is important for the other children already living there. One opportunity for this to happen is through the children being involved in making a video about the home and those who live and work in it, which can be shown to the newcomer.

During the visit the child can be helped to understand why she is moving to her new home, what it is hoped she will achieve and what the plan is for when she leaves. She can be given an outline of her admission plan with details about her visits to the home. How everyone lives together in the home should be explained and thoughts about her initial individual recovery plan should be shared with her, as well as her being given the opportunity to offer her own preferences, established routines and requests. It is useful if a child is able to say what is helpful to her, for it is often the children who know best what they need at certain points in their day. For example, some children will say how they like to be woken up, have their baths prepared, settled at night, and so on. If the child's current routines and rituals can be incorporated into their individual recovery plan this will obviously help bridge their transition into their new home.

Thus, this first visit is a chance to get to know the child: What does she like or dislike? What colours would she like her bedroom to be decorated? What food does she like? At the same time, the child can be offered the opportunity to share something with the children already at the home. For example, is there anything that they could add to the video or send a photograph or a drawing?

This is also a time when the child can be given the chance to send something to her new home to be looked after before she actually arrives. She may well choose something seemingly unimportant but that is not the point. What is important is that it is crucial that when the carer meets the child again he can show how well he has cared for the item. Thus, even in this first meeting the therapeutic relationship with the child has begun: in this first transaction the carer has the opportunity to show the child that he will do as he says and is able to look after something and keep it safe.

The child's visit to the home

After the initial visit to the child, she can then be invited to visit the home accompanied by her current carers or social worker. This visit allows the child a further introduction to the environment and the chance to see that her new carers are reliable and looking forward to her joining them. She will see this by how the carers conduct the claiming process.

This means that before the visit the home will have acted on the information gathered from the visit to the child. For example, the child's bedroom may be painted in the colour chosen by her. The curtains may depict her favourite character; if she wanted a nightlight to help her settle, then one will have been provided. Whatever item she gave the carers to take back to the home before she arrived will have been looked after safely and placed by her new bed. Her photograph may be framed and placed with those of the other children in the home. If the child is to stay for a meal then this could be the meal she said was her favourite. The key carer will be present for all visits by the child to the home. He will join the team looking after all the children.

Initial assessment and initial recovery plan completed

Although a full recovery assessment may not be undertaken until a child has been living at the home for three months, it is important for an initial assessment of need to be carried out to prepare for the child's arrival and initial stay. A team meeting will therefore be held to look at the child's needs and how they will be met when she arrives.

After this, the key carer, supported by senior carers, can produce the initial recovery plan for the team and the child's social worker. It is also prepared for the child in a format that she can understand.

Continuing contact

As well as the planned visits, it is important that the key carer maintains regular contact with the child and her current carers. This can be by telephone, letters, postcards or email. Maintaining this contact will allow the child to feel held in mind throughout the transition period.

An overnight stay by the child in the home

When the child spends a night at her new home, it is important that her new carer will be available throughout the night. Ideally, a third person should also sleep in the home for this night so that the key carer can devote his attention wholly to the new child, rather than also having to deal with the needs of other children in the house. If the accommodation does not allow this, the key carer should focus his attention on the new child and the other carer on the other children. Again, there is an analogy with the good family and the good parent when a new baby arrives and there are other children already in the family. A relative or friend will often come to stay to look after an older brother or sister when a new baby is born.

By now the child's bedroom should be completely decorated and furnished and she knows that this is her room. It is not the case that 'it

doesn't matter' that the bedroom is not fully prepared. The child's first
night in the new home is likely to be an anxious one and a bedroom which
she feels to be her own, decorated and furnished as she wanted it, is part of
that safe and nurturing environment which therapeutic parenting seeks to
provide.

Administration

There are many administrative tasks to be undertaken to support a child's
admission and continuing recovery. It is essential that the child's files are set
up and all individual record books and so on be made up and established in
the home prior to her actual arrival.

Documents should include a personal file (which will include all
referral information as outlined in the referral process and the initial
recovery assessment and recovery plan) to be kept at the home and at
whatever administrative office to which the home is attached if there is one.
There should also be an individual incident recording file held in the home,
as well as a completed impact assessment, agreed and signed by the care
team. Last, the child's name should be added to all group recording
documents.

There has sometimes been a sense that the administration concerning a
child is an unnecessary chore. However, this is something that will again
provide a symbolic claiming and holding of the child. New parents have to
register their babies and complete a whole gambit of administrative tasks. It
seems inevitable and appropriate then that there will be many essential
tasks which formally note the arrival of the new child to a home.

Preparing the other children

As we said at the beginning of this chapter, a child's arrival affects not only
her but also the other children with whom she will be living in the future. It
is important, therefore, that they too are prepared for her coming. A new
child in a home has much greater impact on children who have been abused
than the simple fact of her being 'just' someone else to be accommodated
and adjusted to. For some of these children their relationships with their
brothers and sisters are linked directly with their previous traumatic experiences; for others these relationships were defences against their trauma.

Thus, a new child's arrival may resonate with some of the other children's past and they may need a lot of support to contain the emotions which they may now experience. The use of children's meetings, books and time spent one to one with members of the recovery team should all be seen as opportunities to process those emotions and prepare the children.

On arrival and within the first month

Every new parent knows the practical and emotional consequences of a new arrival in the family, whether it is a first baby or a new brother or sister for an older one. This is no less so with therapeutic parenting. Many of the practical tasks are those that fall to a good parent: registration and appointments with the local GP, dentist and optician; making any additional specialist appointments; visits to begin at the new school or introduction to her new teacher. Dates are planned in the diary for meetings and reviews.

Children coming into residential care require a whole range of statutory plans and meetings: a personal education plan; looked-after children plan; contact arrangements made; reviews; visits, and so on. All this underlines the importance that everything needs to be planned for the child and that she is made aware of this. There should be no surprises for her and everything that is said will happen should take place when she has been told it will. The child can be given a calendar with all significant dates marked and a special box (which should be lockable) made or purchased in which she can choose to place her treasured possessions.

This first month is a busy time for the child when she will be introduced to many new faces and settings. Important among these are her introduction to her life story worker and individual therapist. For many children the therapy and life story aspects of the recovery programme may be new and this first meeting affords an opportunity for her to be introduced to the ideas behind these aspects, when her key carer will be there to give her direct support. It is helpful if the child is able to be shown where her sessions will take place and to have something to take away to promote further discussion back at the home. Leaflets and pictures can be helpful here.

A statutory review will take place after one month which will be attended by the home manager, key carer, therapist and life story worker, and member of the agency's senior management team from the relevant administrative office. As with all reviews, it is important that attention is made to how they are prepared for, conducted, the agenda, the attendance of the child, and what is done afterwards. Reviews can easily become 'professionals' meetings' as they provide a rare opportunity for the adults in a child's life to come together. However, the purpose of a review is to focus directly on the child and should, therefore, at all times be conducted in a manner appropriate to a child being in attendance.

At three months

By this time recovery assessment will have been undertaken with the whole recovery team and an initial recovery plan completed (see Chapter 11). The assessment and plan can be presented within the review report to allow the three-month review to take place.

As well as the practical adjustments that have to be made by her arrival, a new baby can dramatically change the emotional dynamics in a family creating new tensions, challenges and anxieties. This is also the case when a child joins a home. She can bring with her an array of experiences and emotions that will mingle with those already present within the home. Fears, anxieties, jealousy, envy, and so on are all heightened and the containment needed from the carers becomes much greater. Again, as with a family, there will be times when the support of others is needed to help the therapeutic parenting team stay with the struggles and continue with the process of re-parenting the children. The roles of the supervisory relationship, consultancy and team support are crucial to this (see Chapter 4). That an abused child's therapeutic parents experience many of the same emotions and challenges, as well as additional ones, which the parents of a new baby undergo, as well as taking on many of the same kinds of practical tasks, perhaps serves to demonstrate some of the critical elements of how therapeutic parenting works.

Exercises

1. Think about the last time you stayed away from home overnight.

2. What did you miss?

3. What helped to make this experience OK?

4. Imagine you are about to have a child join your household.

5. Write a list of the things you need to do before they arrive and have ready for when they join you.

6. How would your house be changed?

CHAPTER 7

Food for Thought

Food is not only necessary for our very existence but meals have a great social and cultural significance. The formal dinner, family lunch, inviting friends to dinner, meeting for a meal, the celebratory meal for some achievement, an occasion or to lubricate a business meeting – these and other uses of meals testify to the fact that eating serves all kinds of purposes for us as social beings, and at the heart of this is the idea of sharing. Culturally, meals and food are important in other ways – from the Eid midday meal to mark the end of the Ramadan fast for Muslims to Passover for Jews and the traditional Christmas lunch now enjoyed by those of all religions and none. The Catholic mass is itself the liturgical memorial of the Last Supper.

From the first hours of life the importance of food is shown in the relationship between mother and child. The child at the breast is perhaps one of the most natural and comforting images. Babies are completely dependent on their parents for food in order to continue to survive and develop. A mother providing her baby with food therefore represents not only the fulfilment of a physical need but also the baby's total dependence on others for emotional nourishment, validation and nurture. The act of feeding a baby is an essential part of the attachment cycle and crucial to the very early stages of a child's emotional development. Carter (2003) writes:

> As well as the potential to be a mutually pleasurable and satisfying experience the infant can come to experience that there is a world (represented by mother) which understands the anxiety and neediness of hunger and knows how to comfort and take away distress. So the feeding experience can come to represent psychological sustenance

and is part of the infant's developing picture of themselves and the world, and the relation between the two. (p.136)

For us all, then, our earliest infantile experience of feeding and food being provided will not only shape our later relationship with food but also our relationship with others and how we view the world.

Rose (1987) says that 'within such a containing and reconciling environment, food, in particular, becomes invested with great symbolic significance' (p.152). However, he also says that he did not recognize this until he was setting up Peper Harow, a therapeutic community, which he directed for 17 years.

Most children who have been severely abused have been deprived from their earliest years. This will very probably include having had an inadequate or indeed abusive experience of being fed. This can not only affect a child's physical health but will also be part of the regime of deprivation they have suffered which has left them unattached, emotionally frozen or fragmented, with an inner working model which has led to the development of ultimately unhelpful survival strategies. For example, children may become overly self-sufficient so that they cannot accept nurture from someone else. They may gorge on food, taking what they can because they did not know where the next meal was coming from. They may steal or hoard food. They may avoid mealtimes by saying they aren't well or making a fuss at the table, or they may live on a starvation diet because food has unpleasant connotations for them or they feel they cannot rely on it being there.

The need to eat is so primitive that it is often the vehicle for the playing out of emotional disturbance. The concept of eating disorders is an example of this. Obsessively filling oneself with food can be compensation for a lack of love. Anorexia nervosa can be an indication that a person feels no sense of control over their life. While superficially this is sometimes attributed to obsessions about body shape caused by an emphasis in the media on an 'ideal' figure and look, it is likely to go far deeper and be a re-enactment of something earlier in a person's history. For those of a younger age group it may be to do with a young girl's fear of growing up or of becoming like her mother, although this may also be a cause in the illness among older females.

Given the place of food in our earliest of experiences of feeding and relationship, it can provide a very unusual opportunity within a child's recovery programme to meet, symbolically or actually, the missed developmental stages of infancy and rework a child's inner working model. Carers need to think in great detail about all aspects of the provision of food: how it is selected and purchased; how it is stored; what it contains; how it is prepared and presented; its quality and quantity; how it is served at the table; and how leftovers are got rid of. Carers should be aware of the symbolic meaning of food and the conscious and unconscious messages a child may receive and give about how and what is offered.

As food has symbolic as well as actual meaning, it is often used as a means through which children communicate their trauma, transference and distress. Children may reject food as they wish to reject the giver. An offer of food can seem contaminated by the negative feelings they have about the person who offers it. However, Brown (undated) says that it is not always obvious that:

> the emotionally disturbed child who feels undeserving and worthless may have to reject food given in love as being something he doesn't deserve. We are lucky if this happens because we can join the battle to convince the child of his worth, his usefulness, his lovability, in an area which contains our most powerful aids and opportunities for communicating our love and investment in the child. So we fuss and extend ourselves in all the creative ways we can think of. We surround the child with tiny tidbits [sic] and morsels – delicious, appealing, tinged with love, appreciation and the tactful non-verbal communication of our belief in the child's worth. (p.4)

Let us take two everyday matters that have very important implications for how children will perceive they are regarded. First, although most homes will have to work within budgets when purchasing food, what is purchased still needs to be of quality; serving only cheap or convenience, labelled food may give a negative message to a child. Likewise, fruit and vegetables should be fresh and appealing, not thrown into a bag bruised and damaged. Good quality food that is nutritious and aesthetically appealing will allow a child to come to see this as a reflection of her own high worth. Her sense of a lack of self-worth may be reflected in any reliance on pre-prepared meals which are marketed to those who cannot spare the time to cook, or indeed those who can't be bothered. Such food is often less nutritious, of lower quality and less tasty. Perhaps what is being said symbolically to the child is that she isn't worth more and it is not worth making a fuss and caring about what she is given. Food that reflects the cultural and religious preferences of the children being cared for can again reinforce that their individual identities and personalities are valued.

The second common activity that illustrates an important point is about how we purchase and store food: cupboards being full at the start of the week but empty by the end of it can create much anxiety for deprived children. These children may not trust there is enough or that the cupboards will ever be filled again. Such anxiety could lead to a child retreating to previously needed survival techniques such as stealing and hoarding food or gorging on it in an attempt to stock up internally. For some children reassurance can initially come only from their actual seeing there is enough – there is a need for them to know that they will be provided for and so they will compulsively check the fridge and cupboards. Although it is perhaps not possible to replace stock in the cupboards daily, it is possible constantly to replenish the fruit bowl or snack jar which can symbolically give the message to the children that there is and will be enough for all.

We now know that the content of food can affect how children behave (Richardson and Montgomery 2005). Thus carers should pay especial attention to the content of what they buy and be aware of the possible links between additives, colourings, sugar levels and so on and a child's behaviour. With the energetic emergence of 'healthy eating' campaigns there is much support available to carers on such matters.

It is very usual for children from an early age to want to help 'cook' a meal: the pleasure of handling food, the excitement of being helped to put something in the oven or on the boil, the satisfaction of the resultant cake or dish have obvious appeal. For some children such activities can be helpful to support building attachments or as an individual special time. However, this is not helpful for all children. Therefore, cooking should be undertaken only following an assessment of need and as part of a child's individual recovery plan. For example, it may not be helpful for a child to feel compelled to help in providing for others when they are as yet still overwhelmed by their own fear of deprivation. Some children can be too self-sufficient or appear to function much older than their chronological age so that, for example, they ensure that they are fed by being involved in serving food and acting very much like an adult or parent when they would benefit more by having the experience of being provided for by their carers.

Attention to hygiene and safety will help contain the anxieties of those children who fear being poisoned or served food which has been contaminated in some way.

Mealtimes need to be planned, reliable and consistent. They should take place at set times of which the children are made aware in advance. Children should be told beforehand of any changes to the daily routine and be fully informed as to how their meals will be taken. This is particularly important during the school holidays when the daily routine needs to be more flexible to allow for different activities and trips out.

Preparing the dining table is as important as preparing the food. Thought should be given to the use of tablecloths and napkins. Cutlery and crockery should be matched and not be chipped or damaged. Meals should routinely be taken seated at the table with everyone at the home sitting down together. Occasionally, there may be an arrangement, perhaps for the night when a special television programme is to be watched, to eat on laps, but this should not become the norm for any child or home.

For the reasons outlined earlier there should be a sense of plenty and the dining table should always appear full. This can be done by keeping the filled fruit bowl in the centre, providing bread and salad for each meal, and placing jugs of water and juice on the table.

The seating arrangements for both carers and children should be planned in advance and reflect the needs of the children for individual support and the relationships between the children and the carers who are sitting down to eat. Mealtimes are a social event and not just an occasion for eating. They are times when news is swapped and, according to when the meal is taken, the day ahead discussed or the day past mulled over. For many children families coming together have represented conflict and tension which may have led to violence and fear. Food may have been used to humiliate and abuse. It is important, therefore, that mealtimes in the home do not recreate such times for the children. Topics of discussion that may heighten tension or create confrontation are to be avoided and the noise levels kept low. Although they provide an opportunity for communication, mealtimes should not replace other opportunities for group discussion and reflection such as home meetings. Bettelheim (1950) makes a point worth remembering when he writes:

> Mealtime is also a setting which permits us to provide children easily and casually with those infantile pleasures they are anxious to receive but afraid to ask for directly. Children who do not feel secure enough to accept being babied as a matter of course, or to ask for it outright, will manage to create conditions which permit them to enjoy again those pleasurable services which are rightfully due to every infant – services they were prematurely deprived of because their parents forced them to 'act their age' or 'take care of themselves' before they were emotionally ready to do so. (p.200)

What children see on the table reflects their histories and feelings in the same way as we have said they view what is in the fridge and cupboards. Some children will be reassured that they will have enough to eat by the sight of amply filled dishes in the middle of the table. Others may have anxieties that nothing will be left for them if they see other children being served first or serving themselves. Carers serving the food can be both an actual and symbolic demonstration that someone is providing for them. Food already served on a plate when it comes to the table, rather than allowing children to serve themselves, may for some children create the fantasy that what another has got is better or different, that theirs may be less or tarnished in some way.

It may well be impossible to serve in a way that meets the needs of all children but it is important that carers decide on a method for the home which is consistent and reflects an awareness of how children may potentially react to this, given their previous experiences. Children who have been abused and deprived have little, if any, experience of having enough food, which symbolizes their lack of emotional nurture. As a result some will eat too much and some too little, others will hide food. To ensure that they have enough to eat, that it is pleasant, nourishing, well prepared and offered in a way which shows care and attention, is to give them a symbolic sense of a carer's ability to provide enough emotional nurture. The child who eats too much should be encouraged to 'fill' up on healthy alternatives such as a piece of fruit instead of seconds of pudding. As a child develops a healthy attachment with a carer and begins to trust that she will be provided for, she will begin emotionally to 'fill up' and thus not need to try to fill her feeling of emptiness with food.

Food and its provision have often been linked to children's traumatic experiences: it may be food has been used in a sexual manner or as a reward or punishment. It is important for the child to begin to believe that she is entitled to food; that it will always be available to her; and that it will never be used for any ulterior motive or in an unusual way. It should never be locked away.

Carers should not bring their own food and drink into the home because it is important that the children observe that what the home offers is good enough for everyone. Again, for a child where food has been a feature in her trauma this may create fantasies of poisoning, of drugging, or at the very least that she is not worthy of the 'special' food which the carer has.

As the provision of food plays a major role in the development of attachment and symbolically can represent meeting a child's emotional as well as physical needs, each child may benefit from some food provided just for her. This could be special food provided by the key carer, or the carers being aware of a child's likes and dislikes and making provision for this during the main meals. In fact, this is no more than a parent does in knowing his own child's likes and dislikes. A child who is undergoing therapeutic parenting should have her details recorded in her individual recovery plan to ensure that what she is offered by any member of staff is consistent and reliable.

Nothing of what we say here should be taken to mean that children are passive in any of this. With the guidance of carers, they can be involved in the planning and sometimes the preparation of meals. The menu should be a regular item for the children's group meeting to consider. How the good parent treats his child, nurtures her, cares for and protects her, and takes account of her preferences, in matters large and small, is a key to understanding the basis of therapeutic parenting – and this applies critically in matters of mealtimes, food and eating, as in any other areas of the child's life.

Exercises

1. Reflect upon your childhood experiences of food and mealtimes.

2. Do you see any links with these and your relationship with food as an adult?

3. Think about the calendar year.

4. How do you use food to 'mark' or celebrate significant times in the year?

5. Reflect on how food is used and what it contributes to such events.

CHAPTER 8

Someone to be There
The Role of the Key Carer

The key carer is an essential member of the recovery team. While other members of the recovery team – for example, therapists and life story workers – have long-term and close contact with children, he is an active participant in a child's care, not only directly with her but through the work of colleagues and meetings about her. It is the responsibility of the key carer to ensure that colleagues are kept informed of all significant dealings, positive and negative, that the child may have with others. The key carer's connections will go beyond those within his circle of colleagues. He may also need to get to know others and engage with those who are significant in the child's life, for example her parents, brothers, sisters and grandparents. The key carer also sees that the team fully implements the child's individual recovery plan, and that it is also monitored and reviewed.

Given the backgrounds and experiences of traumatized children, the key carer aims first and foremost to be a primary attachment for a child, through which she can experience that maternal preoccupation usually associated with infancy. This is the attachment which, in time, a child may internalize and transfer to future relationships. The safety experienced within this primary attachment will also help the child develop relationships among her contemporaries and to pursue activities outside of the home.

The key carer monitors and supports the child's educational development through close liaison with the school or teachers, attends school meetings, parents' evenings and special events, and makes sure that all the practical arrangements for a child's education are undertaken, such as seeing that she has a uniform. As any good parent, the key carer is interested in the child's progress, asks her about her day, helps with homework and takes an interest in her teachers and friends.

Meeting a child's primary needs is an essential part of the key carer's role. With the support of the therapeutic parenting team he will ensure all aspects of a child's hygiene and physical well-being are looked after: care of her hair; that regular dental visits and health checks are carried out; and that she has a healthy diet. Again, these are as much the tasks of the key carer as the good parent. Likewise, he ensures that those parts of the home personal to the child meet her needs: that her bedroom bears the mark of her own tastes and personality in the way that it is decorated; that it is clean, tidy and well maintained; and that her clothes are kept clean and she is dressed to suit the occasion.

It is through carrying out such seemingly straightforward parental tasks that the key carer can help reformulate the child's sense of self and others. For example, the way in which her clothes are cared for, folded, stored neatly, mended and replaced when necessary tells the child that her possessions are valuable; that how she presents herself is important; that she is worth the time, attention and nurture. For a child whose clothes are thrown willy-nilly into communal washes and left in laundry rooms until found because 'there is nothing else to wear' or which go missing, a very different message is being sent: that what belongs to her is of no value, how she looks doesn't matter, and indeed that she is herself of not much consequence. Through ensuring that the child's possessions are safe and treasured, the key worker is showing her that he can also keep her safe and treasure her.

James: Facing the day

James and his brothers and sisters were never sure if when they woke what kind of day they might face. They slept for most of the day as the night held more terrors for them. They would be left alone. There was no time for them to go to bed or to get up. There were no bedtime stories or gentle music or happy thoughts.

Tomorrow would be as desolate as yesterday and as difficult as today. Theirs was a world of uncertainty, hunger and pain. Their mother, an alcohol-dependent drug user, was unable to attune to the needs of her children who were the result of sexual encounters when she prostituted herself. The home was unkempt, dirty and uncared for, as were her children. Food had become a luxury. When the children woke it could be to their mother being out of it on the settee, or having sex with another drug user. Their pleas for food or other needs would often be met with a harsh violent response.

When James entered therapeutic residential care he found the imposition of routines difficult to cope with. The notion of getting up at a reasonable time was alien to him. He became anxious and displayed this in his disruptive behaviour at night. He stayed awake for much of the night and then refused to get up in the morning, being quite hostile to whoever woke him.

For James, what made an experience in the end worth getting up for was the continual process of being woken gently and thoughtfully, greeted with a smile, chatted to, having someone tidy his clothes away and lay out clean new clothes for the day, telling him what was going to happen and who with, preparing his bath and having breakfast waiting for him, and not being shouted at or hurt. This continued morning after morning, without fail, regardless of how rejecting or uninterested James initially appeared to be.

It cannot be stressed enough how responsible the key carer is for the development of a child's identity and personality, essential as they are to recovery. Thus, he will see that her cultural needs are met and that she is able to follow her religion if she has one. He will know about the significant events in her year which she will want to celebrate, as well as those events which may resonate with her previous traumatic experiences and cause her distress and anxiety and for which she may need additional understanding and support.

It is also part of the role of the key carer to ensure that other parts of the recovery areas are available to the child and that she takes part in them. This may mean that the key carer ensures that she attends therapy and life story sessions, as well as supporting the child with any emotional ambivalence she may have by attending the programme. The key carer or at least a supporting carer should accompany the child to her sessions and so be able to ensure the security of their relationship before and after the session. The key carer can play a very significant role in life story work, engaging with the child and the life story worker in the life story journey (Rose and Philpot 2005). The key carer, like a parent, is in the best position to gather and collate a record of the child's time with the agency through photographs, certificates and memorabilia.

Maternal preoccupation

Being a new parent is a frequently exhausting and all-absorbing task. Whatever one may want to do oneself often has to be put aside to meet a baby's very basic needs – for food, sleep, toileting, and so on. A child crying for its food or wanting a nappy changed can't be ignored so that the chapter of a book can be finished, the lawn cut or a quick visit made to the shops. Her needs have to be met there and then. Indeed, the complete dependency of the baby and small child on a parent means that parents not only have to respond to what their child needs but they are also required to predict and pre-empt what she cannot communicate. The parent – most commonly the mother – becomes of necessity preoccupied.

As we have mentioned above, the key carer aims to develop and offer the child an experience of having someone preoccupied with her and attuned to her needs. What Winnicott (1992) called 'primary maternal preoccupation' is the state which he likened to an illness afflicting a healthy mother but which had to occur to facilitate the child's health. It was, he said, a 'state of heightened sensitivity, almost an illness' from which, eventually, the infant 'releases' her (p.302). He goes on to state that it:

> provides a setting for the infant's constitution to begin to make itself evident, for the developmental tendencies to start to unfold, and for the infant to experience spontaneous movement and become the owner of the sensations that are appropriate to this early phase of life. (p.303)

As Winnicott (1992) futher explains:

> Only if the mother is sensitized in the way I am describing can she feel herself into her infant's place, and so meet the infant's needs. These are at first body needs, and they gradually become ego needs as a psychology emerges out of the imaginative exploration of physical experience.
>
> There comes into existence an ego-relatedness between mother and baby, from which the mother recovers, and out of which the infant may eventually build the idea of a person in the mother. From this angle the recognition of the mother as a person comes in a positive way, normally, and not out of the experience of the mother as the symbol of frustration. (p.303)

Winnicott dated this period of preoccupation, or as he preferred to say the mother being 'given over to' the care of her baby (Winnicott 1990), as being from the end of pregnancy for a few weeks after birth. Of course, babies and small children are dependent for much longer than that but Winnicott is concerned to explain this initial period of utter dependence, this almost melding together of the life of the mother and that of her baby before the mother is 'released' from her 'illness'.

Dockar-Drysdale (1968) said that the common factor she noted in the different kinds of traumatized children with whom she worked was the interruption of the unity of mother and baby in the immediate postnatal period. She put this down to the 'premature failure' of mothers or mother-substitutes in adapting to their babies' needs in the first year of life (p.101). Dockar-Drysdale's belief was that interruption leads to much emotional deprivation. The failure could come about in different ways: a mother may be unable to be preoccupied with her baby for a sufficiently long time; she might experience initial fusion with the child but separation only comes about by withdrawal of concern; there may be an actual separation between mother and baby; or the father, normally the protector of the vulnerable unit, may be absent or have died.

The concept of maternal preoccupation can be applied to those children whom we refer to as severely traumatized. It is likely that they will have been denied this very basic human relationship from the time of their birth. This then results (as described in Chapter 2) in an attachment either not having taken place or one which has occurred but has been seriously impaired. The key carer and the therapeutic parenting team seek, therefore, to offer the opportunity for a child to receive such attention and to experience this unmet developmental need. In doing so the carer has to replicate, as close as is practicable, the maternal preoccupation which characterizes the healthy parent–child relationship. As we said earlier, this is done through the key carer being attuned to all of a child's emotional and practical life. He will be able to know, predict, prepare in advance, empathize, ensure, provide, as well as be open to and survive the unknown and the element of surprise.

Maternal preoccupation is a key practice in therapeutic parenting. A child's relationship with her key carer helps her to have the experiences necessary to feel that she is separate from that person, a vital step in developing a sense of her own identity. Eventually, children develop a sense of empathy, the essential ingredient in our relationship with others: to see and understand how our behaviour and that of others affects them and how they in turn affect others. The key carer has a critical part to play in allowing a child to develop such empathy, crucial for her recovery and for finally being able to take her place in the world.

Exercises

1. Reflecting upon your own experiences as a parent or by imagining you now care for a child, write a job description and person specification for this role. Include both the practical and emotional components of the role.

2. Now imagine you care for a traumatized child. Is there anything different in the job description or person specification?

CHAPTER 9

A Chance to Grow

Meeting a Child's Developmental Needs

One of the most significant effects on children who have been traumatized through abuse is upon their development. As Tomlinson (2004) explains:

> A traumatized child needs to make sense of the trauma so that it can be put into perspective. The shock of the trauma can cause a regression in the child's development. A person who is in shock cannot think or attend to ordinary things. Regression can be a defensive falling back to trigger a supportive and protective response from others. This aspect of trauma leads to the need for both understanding and nurture. The nurture is necessary to fill the gap in development that has been created and to establish a sense of security that makes it safe to move forwards again. (p.16)

According to Balbernie (1989), therapeutic parenting seeks to provide a:

> corrective emotional experience when something missed out on once can be either directly or symbolically experienced in a substitute setting. This has greater effect when the client can abandon rigid and inappropriate defences and feel able to relax back in touch with regressive longings and act upon them. For these processes to occur there needs to be an environment that firmly offers safety and can be trusted. (p.6)

By offering a clearly defined and consistent structure of roles, daily routines and behavioural expectations and a recovery team able to offer emotionally secure and trusting relationships, the therapeutic parenting team provides a psychologically holding environment through which understanding, growth and change can occur. Balbernie (1973) explains: 'If there is a sense of being contained safely by a caring structure that can survive unchanged, however much attacked, then new (untested, unknown and thus unsafe) abilities and personality functions can emerge and be experimented with' (p.7).

Often when a child joins a placement she has a need to establish communication and make her emotional state felt. However, most children are not able to communicate with words about how frightened and awful they may feel. In which case, they will often communicate by projective identification, the projecting of part of themselves, the frightened fearful self, into others. They often do this through behaviours and actions that cause others around them to feel such feelings themselves. Part of the healing task is for the recovery team to contain these painful emotions of the children.

Many of the children coming into placement try to re-create situations from their past, not only because they often feel that it is safer to do this in that it is a known situation, but also because it serves to communicate to the new carers a real sense of their trauma. Jack, for example, recalled a memory of being dropped by his mother from a high-rise flat when he was an infant. The memory seemed to represent his feelings of being 'dropped' emotionally by his mother and his loss of her. In the early days of his treatment if he was left alone, Jack would frequently be found to have broken window latches or indeed windows and be sitting on a ledge at risk of falling. In team meetings the carers described the intense feelings of fear and anxiety they experienced when they found him like this. They feared he would fall and they would lose him. Through his re-creation Jack enabled the carers to have a 'real' sense of his own traumatic experience. The carers' ability to tolerate, put into words and process their feelings at these points and not lose Jack (perhaps to a more secure placement) were internalized by him and led to his being able to 'hold on' to his new relationships.

The quality of communication and interaction with a child throughout her placement is crucial in providing experiences which will help counteract her previous view of herself and others. Children who are looked after by others often believe they are not with their birth families because they were born so awful that their families couldn't bear them and therefore rejected them. They may believe that the cause of their trauma was their intrinsic badness and their own fault. According to Lanyado (1991):

> Sexually abused children frequently have a powerful sense of their own badness. It is as if they feel full of bad substances, memories and fantasies, to the extent that they quite literally are 'bad' – with no other internal experiences to moderate the intensity of their self-destruction and sadism. (p.136)

In thinking about a child's behaviour as a communication to us we are able to communicate with her in a thoughtful way and make attempts to understand and respond to what is being communicated.

In the case of Jesse, after a difficult confrontation over a seemingly minor incident she went to her bedroom and began to throw and break things. The carer went to Jesse's room, knocked on the door, said that he was concerned for Jesse's safety and that he would be entering. Upon entering the carer observed that there were belongings scattered over the floor and a few significant items broken – the room looked very messy. The carer told Jesse what he saw and tried to relate this to what she may have been communicating, 'There's quite a mess in here, perhaps you sometimes feel messy inside. A few things seem to be broken, destroyed or damaged.'

When the carer offered to clear things up for Jesse, she agreed. This was undertaken carefully and throughout the carer asked Jesse where and how she would like things to be, and what perhaps needed to be thrown away or vacuumed up. After the clearing up was complete Jesse said that she felt better.

There were, though, several other things that the carer could have done. He could have stormed into Jesse's bedroom and immediately stopped her from doing more damage. He could have walked into the room and insisted she clear up the mess she had made. He could have insisted she put her feelings into words and pressurized her to 'tell me all about it'. These options are commonplace and might have had the desired effect of stopping the action and getting things back to where they were. However, the response the carer did make enabled a therapeutic dialogue to take place. Although neither Jesse nor the carer talked about feelings directly, a communication took place which the carer then tried to make sense of and give words to. After the communication Jesse made it known that she felt better. Although perhaps she was not aware of the symbolic nature of the act it was felt internally and unconsciously to be containing.

Regression

It is perhaps not surprising that when the children we describe in this book have reached a point where attachments are forming they should start to regress. Indeed, for a child who has not known maternal preoccupation, who has lacked attachments, regression is a means of seeking what was lost or what was not known and experienced at an earlier stage of life. It is 'a search for missing relationships' as Tomlinson (2004, p.27) calls it. These children have not had a 'good enough' adaptation to their needs in infancy and so there is now a need for symbolic and sometimes actual adaptations to offer that provision and relationship which has been missed.

Tomlinson (2004) makes use of the term 'adaptations' or 'adaptation to need' when discussing actual and symbolic provision. It is something, he says, which is central to the therapeutic approach of Dockar-Drysdale (1990a). It can, he writes, 'be provided in any setting where a child has the need for primary provision because of early childhood trauma and deprivation' (pp.26–27). He goes on to say that adaptation is the means by which children who have been denied the 'good enough' adaptations in infancy – which allows the infant the illusion of being in control and omnipotent – and have regressed can have their needs met appropriately. But he also states:

> The adaptation has an 'as if' quality to it and if it becomes too close to the actual thing, it loses this quality and becomes more like an actual substitute. A baby's bottle feels too close to the actual provision for a baby to maintain an 'as if' quality. It could feel that we are trying to provide a substitute experience. If this were the case, it would not be a useful provision. It would be difficult for the provision to remain localized as it may feel that we were offering the child the opportunity to really be a baby. We need to hold onto the reality that we cannot actually provide this experience. (p.28)

Regressive needs can also come as a result of the shock of trauma. It can be a way of seeking help and protection and thus is best dealt with by responding directly to this. The sense of security that results is one which allows the child to move forward again, just as the regressed, unattached child can move towards maturity by nurturing and provision which fill the gaps in her development.

Regression can be seen as the confirmation of hope for the child's recovery. It occurs when a child has begun to accept provision from the carers and begins to initiate the meeting of their previously unmet infantile needs. Regression in the residential setting is similar to that which may take place in a therapy session in that it is confined to time limits, location and particular relationships: it is localized. Localized regression enables a child to have her early needs met at the same time as she continues to function in her chronologically appropriate reality.

A child regressing will communicate her need for her earlier needs to be met through the way in which she behaves. For example, she may stop being able to do some things for herself and revert to points before key stages of development. As the child regresses the therapeutic parenting team attempt to meet her needs, both symbolically and sometimes actually.

To take another example, a child may be provided, without prompt or request, with a 'special' drink in a 'special' cup at bedtime. She may be read a bedtime story, although quite able to read herself. She may have her bed folded back before she goes upstairs. A 14-year-old may have hot milk and biscuits in bed or she might communicate through her teddy bear, with teddy being put to bed and teddy discussing what it will do tomorrow.

Teenagers, to take another example, are not usually tucked up at night by their parents, but this may be just the right thing for certain children in that age group who have never experienced the kind of loving and parental concern which tucking up represents. Most 15-year-olds may be encouraged to put their clothes away and not wait for their parents to pick them up and put them in the drawer, wardrobe or washing machine. However, a carer may undertake all these chores for a 15-year-old who seems no longer able to do this. However, as we have explained earlier, there are of course limits to how a carer can offer maternal preoccupation to an older child.

Individual provision and special times

Individual provision aims to meet the individual needs of a child, and a special time takes the child out of the general provision and the life she ordinarily shares with other children. It is usually about a very commonplace thing: a meal, a chance to play, bathtime. It might be done, for example, by the key carer always getting the child's comic for her on a Friday, but if he goes on holiday he ensures that someone else does that job. Thus, the Friday comic offers the child a routine, consistency (she knows that she will get the comic) and, perhaps most significantly, the fact that even though he is going on holiday the key carer has thought to ensure that the child is important enough for him to think of her. This directly challenges the child's inner working model which tells her that she has no value and that adults cannot be trusted. A sense of trust is important in developing a sense of identity. Even a seemingly small action, like making sure the comic is bought every week, is one small way of helping a child to build that trust. Such an action also allows the adult to think about the child's needs and to understand her view of the way the world works.

David: The birthday boy

David is the youngest of six children. His mother is heroin dependent with a life style that has been for many years chaotic. She is often homeless and involved in criminal activity to fund her habit. She has lived in squats with male drug users. David's father, of whom David has little or no memory, is in prison for sexual offences against children, although not against his son.

David and his sister would often be found shoplifting from the local supermarket. As the children were below the age of criminal responsibility no action was taken against them. Their mother would sell the stolen goods to fund her habit. The local communities became quite hostile towards the family and they moved on numerous occasions.

David had over 15 different placements before being received into care full time. He then had a further 23 placements, some of a short-term nature, before his final placement.

He was a very angry young boy who pushed boundaries constantly and wanted to be in control of situations. If he was challenged about his behaviour or asked to do something he did not want to do he would become very destructive, breaking windows, furniture or any items given to him, and physically attacking the adults and any children in the vicinity. He was disruptive, argumentative and self-harmed by head banging and throwing himself around the room without thought for his safety or that of others.

Although boundaries could be placed around David to keep him safe and protect others, the full extent of the deprivation, anger and pain he had suffered was not appreciated until it came close to his birthday. While discussing what he might want for his birthday David seemed to ask for things that he didn't really like. His carers' practice was to find a range of things a child might like and then choose items from this list as a surprise.

As his birthday approached David's behaviour became even more aggressive and destructive. By spending time with him and talking about his birthday, the party, the food and his guests, and helping him to make choices, anticipate his anxieties and demonstrate that his birthday was important to those who cared for him, David was able to let it be known that he had never really celebrated a special time before. He eventually said that he didn't care what he got as he had always had whatever presents there had been in the past removed from him either through his behaviour or his mother would sell them for drugs.

David's feelings of worthlessness had been contributed to by the fact that, like so many abused children, he had been denied those special times like birthdays, anniversaries and Christmas which most of us take for granted. With thoughtful and patient work, David had lots of presents that he wanted. He was reassured that he could keep them and was able to experience an enjoyable birthday for probably the first time.

Individual provision can also be a special time when other carers and children do not intrude on the time of the carer, taking his attention away from the child. It is a time, then, when the carer is wholly focused on one child, is deeply maternally preoccupied. To do so, he will need to be finely attuned to the child's inner needs.

But while one carer concentrates on one child to the exclusion of all else for a specified period of time that is ruthlessly protected, this is not something which is done in isolation. As has been said, the whole experience and emotional and physical environment in which therapeutic parenting takes place is therapeutic and individual provision is no exception. This special time is supported by all members of the recovery team, who will learn from it and contribute to it, if only by ensuring, for example, that other children do not seek the attention of the key carer or try to make contact with the child during this period. Team members will also be aware of any negative feelings arising on the part of other children because of the individual provision given to one child. They can help to resolve and overcome them. Problems that can arise as a result of individual provision may be felt not only by the other children but also by the child being individually provided for. While individual provision is a carer being one to one with a child, that child may be strongly attached to more than one carer and may wish the other to be involved as well, or wish that the second and not the first was the individual provider. Children may try to play one carer off against the other, or position one as good and the other as bad. Without acknowledgement and understanding of such dynamics the team could quickly be caught up in unhelpful behaviours and are likely to re-enact a child's previous history.

Lucas (1992), writing from the perspective of her work at the Mulberry Bush School, quotes the dilemma raised by Maier (1985) which she personally has experienced. Maier wrote: 'Group care workers tend to be caught between…opposing demands such as being fully engaged with all children and being especially attentive to children who require individual adult involvement.' Lucas explains that her experience has been that at times she has been asked to shorten the special time so that she can be available to a group of children. She has also felt anxiety that there were not sufficient carers available when she was supposed to be engaged with a child's individual provision. This provoked in her feelings of guilt towards the child for not being able to fulfil her needs adequately, while at the same time experiencing anger towards the senior colleague seeking to curtail the special time. Such a situation not only deprives the child of adequate special provision (thus, of course, indicating to her that the carer is unreliable and her needs are secondary), but also she may well pick up the negative feelings affecting the carer. The carer may be placed in a negative frame of mind towards both the child and a colleague, and possibly the agency for which he works – after all, doesn't the agency have overall responsibility for what happens?

Lucas makes a very positive point when she goes on to say that, accepting the dilemma and her feelings, she has always found it possible to discuss what has happened with the colleague concerned, which has led to the feelings between them being relieved. This points again to the need for any work to be carried out against a background of openness between colleagues and regular, skilled supervision being available.

Outside of special times, the child will be 'sharing' her special carer with other children at meals and other times. Lucas (1992), drawing on earlier writings by Dockar-Drysdale (1968) on the importance of role and function, points to the two roles in which the child will know that adult: one in a 'maternal' role when he is preoccupied with her and the other in a 'paternal' role when he is responsible for setting boundaries, discipline, and so on. Children, of course, are used to carers playing different roles. However, jealousy, rejection, loss and rivalry may still be present as they can be with the best adjusted child in certain situations. For the abused child it may not be the situation as such which gives rise to intense emotions but the transference of feelings stemming from past trauma that are brought into the present.

In such situations it is important to understand what children are experiencing and why – the more so when there appears to be no apparent cause. The carer who is the 'cause' of the behaviour may need the practical support of colleagues. This is an important indicator to the child, as to the carer, that individual provision is not a thing apart from the total environment, but something which is offered within it.

The child in the group

All of us are individuals and all of us will have (indeed continue to have) some kind of group experience, some more intense or intimate than others

– the family, the school, the workplace, a cricket club, a political party, and so on. The first experience of the group that most children understand is that of their family, good or bad as it may be. Even children whose welfare demands that they be removed from their families are placed in another kind of group – be it a foster or adoptive family or residential care.

In a healthy family a child grows to have a sense of her own identity and to learn her place and role in relation to others, which then extends to how she behaves in the wider community. A child learns these lessons partly by mixing with other members of the group as well as knowing them as individuals – her brothers and sisters and parents, the extended family. When she goes to school (or earlier at nursery school), the same applies. She meets her contemporaries (as well as the teachers) as a group but she also mixes with them as individuals. She is discovering, for example, how she will accommodate herself to what her mother or father may tell her to do; or how she will resolve the conflicts she feels with having an older brother or sister or a younger child if it comes along. How will she learn to live with children whom she doesn't know so well at school? How will she fall in with the discipline which the teacher imposes?

We sometimes think of the family group as a microcosm of the wider world and how it works as a preparation to enter wider worlds, both as a child, an adolescent and, finally, as an adult. This may mean perhaps that we sometimes overlook the fact that, even in families where there is more than one child, all children receive individual attention and care. This is obvious when we think of a birth in the family. If it is the first child, then parents (particularly the mother) can focus their attention exclusively on the new arrival. But even where the new baby is an addition, while parents do not neglect her brothers and sisters they need to concentrate much attention on the new arrival. At the same time, parents will also make a point of seeing that another child does not feel overlooked or neglected and even give them special treats. For example, while Mummy looks after baby Jane, Daddy will take little Johnny to the park.

While therapeutic parenting, by the nature of its task, is more structured than family life, which can often feel quite spontaneous even when it isn't, children in need of therapeutic parenting are helped by both group living and individual provision. Just as attempting to meet the needs of individual children within the family can evoke unintended jealousies and tensions among other children, so individual provision is not without problems to overcome or seek to avoid.

Exercises

We often assume we know what is 'normal' in relation to a child's development, what age they should reach milestones such as sitting up, first words, first lost tooth, playing by rules, etc. Put yourself to the test.

1. Write five significant things you may observe about a child for each year from birth to eight.

2. How does your list compare with others?

CHAPTER 10

The Means to Recovery

Effective assessment is an essential part of an integrated approach to treating traumatized children, for, as Ward (2004) says, one 'can have assessment without treatment, but you certainly can't have treatment without assessment'.

If therapeutic parenting is a means of compensating for the deficiencies in a child's experience of parenting, or indeed lack of parenting, then assessment will identify what these deficiencies are so it needs to be undertaken at an early stage in the child's placement. Ward (2004) goes on to describe assessment as a 'process of making sense of current available experience, to help you have some idea of what is going on in your interactions with the child, in order that you may modify, interrupt, emphasize or even ignore certain aspects of the dynamic'.

The assessment is about gathering essential information and understanding the child's current experience, but we also need to have a thorough and detailed knowledge of a child's history and previous experience.

Thus, investigating the child's past can help identify the nature of her trauma, which basic needs were met and which were not; provide birth details which may have had an impact on her development; outline the stages of development, achievement of milestones or the failure to achieve them; and help to identify what abuse may have occurred. Piecing together her history may help us to understand how the child is likely to respond to new carers because of her past experience, as well as providing clues about the child's perceptions of current events. It may alert us to events which may trigger off strong feelings and responses, as well as identifying how the child has coped with stress in the past. Fahlberg (1994) sums up succinctly the way a child's mind works. This needs to be grasped when undertaking assessment. She writes:

> Children, particularly young children, believe that their lives are 'normal'. They are incapable of comparing their own situation with that of others. They incorporate their own experiences into their overall view of what family life is like and take these perceptions and their own reactions to them into any new settings. (p.232)

From the investigation, patterns will emerge: behaviour patterns and those which have precipitated placement breakdowns. We will come to know of anniversaries and incidents, and re-creations of a situation or a relationship from the child's past. We will have an idea of the child's education, as well as how she has coped socially, for example, when she has lived in groups. The family history may identify family patterns, scripts and the history of relationships with others (Rose and Philpot 2005).

SACCS has developed an internal assessment process that draws together these essential elements of past and present and gives priority to the sharing of information and insights that each element may provide. Current information and experience is taken from all three areas of the recovery programme, thus integrating therapeutic parenting, life story and therapy (Rymaszewska and Philpot 2006).

If we regard recovery as a journey, then assessment is something which allows us to chart how far along the road the child has travelled. In drawing that map, we need to include a definition of what the end of the journey will be like: what is the destination we are aiming for? In developing a recovery assessment it is necessary, therefore, to develop that definition and to know how we can recognize its achievement.

SACCS' assessment model begins with identifying what is meant by recovery. This is when the child has internalized her attachments and consolidated her emotional development to a point where these can be successfully transferred to other environments and relationships. The child is then deemed to have the potential to achieve to full ability in all aspects of her life.

Twenty-four outcomes have been set by SACCS which recognize that recovery has been achieved. These are quoted below. If a child is able to demonstrate she is reaching these outcomes it is felt she would most likely have reached the point of recovery as described. The outcomes are when a child:

- **has a sense of self of whom she is and where she has been.** This means that the child has a sense of her own identity and culture, regardless of creed, race, nationality, or religion, especially if there are also issues of disability and/or gender. She understands about her family of origin, has worked through what she loves, hates, is angry about, is frightened of, and is not in denial. She knows who she is in relationship to important people in her past and significant people in her present. She has integrated her past experiences into her present reality. Her personality is clear and intact. The child is living mostly in the present. Her past is no longer controlling her life.

- **has an understanding of her past history and experiences.** That is she has thoroughly worked through the issues and trauma in her past and has understood what has happened to her, when and in what order with her current cognitive ability. The child has some insights about how her past experiences impact on her present behaviour. Her internal working model of the world has expanded to incorporate new models of how to be.

- **is able to show appropriate reactions.** She can recognize her feelings accurately and her behaviour is able to convey that feeling to others, so that she feels sad and doesn't laugh, or feels frightened and doesn't put herself into more dangerous situations, or feels angry and wants to be loving. She is able to feel love and be loving, feel the pain and be sad, feel rage and be angry, and feel frightened and be scared.

- **has developed internal controls** and thus is able to recognize what is right and what is wrong and wants to regulate her behaviour herself within what is considered acceptable. External controls, boundaries and supervision no longer have to be so intense, and the child has built up a level of trust with her carers, and is confident that she will be able to contain her feelings and behaviour.

- **is able to make use of opportunities** so that she is no longer a victim of the world, but is now a survivor, recognizing possibilities and opportunities when they arise and is able to put herself forward to take advantage of those possibilities. It also means being able to ask for what she wants. It does not mean using opportunities to overwhelm and victimize other children, or to break the law in any other way.

- **is able to make appropriate choices** so that she is no longer a victim and able to recognize that she has choices available to her and that she is actually already exercising those choices. She is able to see that she has a future and can have an active role in shaping it, which can take a number of different forms. It also means that the choices that the child is able to make promote physical and emotional health.

- **is able to make appropriate adult and peer relationships.** She is able to recognize that she is a child of appropriate chronological age and is able to function at that age. The relationships and attachments that the child is able to make are appropriate to the situation. She is able to recognize that past relationships have been distorted through abusive or neglectful experiences.

- **is able to make academic progress** so that she is able to achieve her potential within her intellectual ability. It may mean that as the child becomes clearer, she is, therefore, better able to concentrate and to perform more productively within the range of ability. She is more able to get totally involved in tasks in the present, for example reading a story, and less involved with ruminating about negative things in the past.

- **is able to take responsibility** and is no longer in denial about her past. She apportions blame appropriately and if it is part of her story is able to see her part in what happened. Taking responsibility implies being able to make choices, and being aware of them and any consequences that may occur as a result of that particular choice being made. Therefore the child is able to make a decision about what is to happen, knowing and accepting the result whatever it might be.

- **has developed conscience** and, thus, a sense of right and wrong, and is able to feel remorse if she has hurt someone or something. This can only be done in the context of a significant and safe relationship or attachment.

- **is no longer hurting herself or others.** This means that she is not physically, sexually, verbally, emotionally or intellectually victimizing other children or adults. Nor is she harming herself, physically, sexually, verbally, emotionally or intellectually. She recognizes that she is a valuable human being worthy of respect, and prepared to be respectful. She also understands that animals are not objects of physical or sexual torture or harm.

- **is developing insights.** Through an understanding of her past experiences, when it no longer has any power over her behaviour, thoughts and feelings, only then is the child able to see objectively who she is, and who significant others are, in relationship to her. Importantly, she is able to see her victimization not as something which she made happen, but rather the person who victimized her actively planned; she just happened to be there. She is then able to see the role of whatever adults were involved either in harming her or not protecting her or both.

- **has completed important developmental tasks.** When a child has been traumatized through abuse, she is sometimes 'pseudo-mature', or a preoccupation with the abusive relationship means that important developmental tasks have not been completed. The child will need to revisit these stages and ages in order to complete these tasks successfully so that she is able emotionally to grow up and achieve self-mastery. It also means that the adults around her are prepared to allow her to be the age she is now, to regress if needed to an earlier developmental stage, to acknowledge that and support it, and to help the child feel safe enough to do this work, and respect and affirm its importance.

- **has developed cause and effect thinking** so that she understands that when she does something there is a consequence, good, bad or indifferent. This implies that the child is able to make choices and to see that other people and other people's feelings and possessions matter. It also implies that she is able to think logically, and linearly, and is not egocentric.

- **understands sequences**. The child understands not only about cause and effect, and her part in it, but also about how one thing follows on from another, or leads to it and why. She is able to see links in a set of circumstances and a logical understanding of why this happens.

- **has developed motor skills** whereby she has met all her developmental milestones. She is less self-absorbed and much more aware of the space she has taken up in the world and her relationship to it. She is also much more able to concentrate on tasks, and be less lost in the past.

- **has developed abstract thinking** so that she is able to conceptualize without the object being in front of her. This is also an ability to represent symbolically her experience and distress and to get resolution through these symbolic representations.

- **has improved physical health** because she is receiving sufficient care and nurture, and safety. Her body and her spirit are able to recover their full potential.

- **has normal sleeping habits.** She will understand that going to sleep is a healthy, safe, necessary and lovely thing to do and doing this at the proper time is a prerequisite to normal functioning. The child does not have to be responsible for ensuring she has a safe night's sleep. She understands, too, that the rest of the world also sleeps at that time, which creates an understanding that there is time for everything: there will be a time for all her needs to be met. Structure and routine, being imposed by adults who care about them, is the beginning of a relationship and/or attachment.

- **has normal personal hygiene.** She will have sufficient respect for herself that she wants to look after her body and bodily functions in the best way that she can. We need to understand that when traumatized children do not care for themselves, soil, smear or wet themselves, they are actually showing their pain, and not being disgusting, but rather showing us how disgusting they think they are. Traumatized children learn that their bodies are not worthy of respect or care and that means that they themselves are not worthy of respect or care. Adults who keep them safe, care and nurture them are able to teach them how to love and respect themselves within a trusting relationship.

- **has normal eating behaviours**, which means that she no longer has to overeat or refuse food for reasons linked to her past abuse, or either to comfort herself or harm herself. She may lack the skills to feed appropriately, and will learn these through a safe and loving relationship.

- **has normal body language**, which means that she develops awareness of how she is using her body to communicate to adults and those of her own age. This implies that she is aware of her own feelings and knows how to show them appropriately. It also means that she understands about acceptable touching, and her personal space and that of others. It is an awareness of what kind of touch is acceptable and loving, and what is not. It is an ability to use the language of their bodies, and to know what she is communicating to others.

- **has normal self-image.** She is able to acknowledge that she is as she is. She sees herself as others see her. She can acknowledge her strengths as well as being realistically aware of her weaknesses. The abused child carries a mental picture which is an image in her mind of her body which may be distorted as a result of past trauma. She is aware of the space she takes up in the world and her relatedness to everything around her. It is only when she can see herself through the eyes of significant people who love her that she can start to love herself.

- **is able to make positive contributions:** to respect herself and her opinions as a creative force. She is able to ask for what she wants, and intervenes appropriately in a positive way in other interactions. She is able to view the world as a healthy, safe and exciting place that she has a part in creating and influencing.

(Walsh 2002)

These outcomes are grouped together under the areas of:

- learning
- physical development
- emotional development
- attachment
- identity
- social and communicative development.

While, as we have said, it is important to gather all we can of the child's current and previous details for an informed assessment, it is perhaps just as important how this information is brought together, shared and then used. For a recovery programme aiming to integrate all aspects of a child's life in placement and treatment, the development of an integrated assessment model is crucial. It is therefore worth describing this model.

An integrated approach

The integrated model contains a large number of key aspects that underpin the assessment process. These include lines of communication between all members of the recovery team always being open and clearly defined. Communications should flow between the therapeutic parenting team, the therapist and life story workers. In addition, all members of the child's recovery team should appraise, update and share new insights, strategies or anxieties with the referring local authority that may occur between reviews or designated contact visits on a regular basis.

Others who are not working directly with the child have their part to play in her recovery so it is essential that teachers at the child's school should be involved and brought up to date with all significant events, behavioural changes or any issue that the recovery team feels will affect the child's ability to focus and contribute to school life.

The communication and reflective thinking about a child should be very detailed. A seemingly unimportant comment from a child can often, when placed in a wider context, together with other people's information and insights, make sense in a way it could never do when it was only an isolated utterance.

One of the main tasks of the life story team is to act as psycho-therapeutic detectives (Rose and Philpot 2005). As we have said, the recovery team will piece together what is currently known about a child, following subsequent discoveries unearthed by the life story team, including sharing with the team any new interview with a significant person in the child's life.

The recovery team must meet regularly to discuss each child and to probe and debate facts and beliefs that are held about her. Recovery assessments offer another forum for the combined team to ask questions about the child and develop a shared language and construct a way of working with the child to achieve her maximum potential to recover.

The recovery team must think about the child together in order to understand her better. The team must identify where a child has reached in her emotional development. A child should be held collectively in mind and the impact of her trauma on the six areas of functioning outlined above should be considered.

Integrated working provides the team with a means of tracking progress or highlighting areas of major concern if their scoring scale unpredictably slips or dips from previous scaling. It also identifies blocks and looks to other members of the team to offer fresh insights or suggestions for strategies in order to move the child forward. Integrated working offers a potentially creative space for any member of the recovery team to air and reflect upon feelings that the child evokes in them.

The child's internal working model should be analysed and a working hypothesis made of what impact this may have on how a child views herself as well as her relationship with the world around her. Strategies, beliefs and interventions should be evaluated, and a consensus needs to be reached about what works and what does not.

The team will learn a great deal from exploration of the feelings evoked in them through being with the child as their feelings can be a projection of what the child herself is feeling and, therefore, if reflected upon can teach us much about the child at that point in time. Flynn (1998) refers to 'a culture of inquiry' fostering 'creative and containing work' (p.167).

Everyone concerned with the child's recovery should meet every six months at a meeting chaired by an independent senior practitioner. Those working in therapy, life story and therapeutic parenting should be asked to score or scale the child, independently of each other; the areas under observation representing six areas of functioning, on which trauma has had a direct or indirect impact.

When the various scores are transferred to a chart this allows focus and analysis in order to produce new strategies for the team's work or for it to continue if the child is making progress. Drift is avoided by plotting a child's progress like this, as well as helping all team members to think more clearly. It is also a method of finding out where the child is on her road to recovery. Any new behaviours or any new information that has come to light recently can be communicated and woven into the proposed strategy of interventions. The recovery team should be encouraged at the meetings to say what they feel about the child and how they view her.

They should be able to talk about their struggle to absorb the bombardment of powerful projections they receive from the child and how they interpret their countertransference. Matters like envy or resentment between team roles can be aired. Feelings of being attacked, either mentally or physically, can be shared with the group and their support sought if they are experiencing exhaustion or ambivalence.

The six-monthly meeting, then, offers the opportunity for the team to consider their work together, with the support of the chairperson, so that there is an increased understanding of the child. An individual recovery plan will be developed after each assessment. The plan identifies key aspects of a child's daily living, relationships and engagement in therapy and life story that warrant individual and more intensive focus and intervention. The assessment thus informs and is realized in the treatment plan.

Both assessments and the plans emerge by the team allowing the child's needs to be identified, monitored and met consistently and systematically at each child's own pace. Alvarez (1992) reminds us that 'recovery can be a long, slow process, particularly for the children who have been abused chronically at a young age' (p.151). Working with traumatized children is both complex and time consuming and needs to be underwritten by the utmost sensitivity. The recovery plan is a means by which a team can ensure consistency in their approach to the child as she makes that journey towards recovery.

Exercises

We have highlighted the importance of a child's history in relation to the assessment of their needs.

1. Write a list of the information you feel would enable a carer to have a real sense of a child's history.

2. Now write a list of the current information you would need to complement the history in an assessment.

3. Within your current role how would you go about gathering such information?

4. Reflect upon the child or children you care for.

5. What is it you are hoping to achieve with and for them?

6. Write a definition (as we have done for a recovered child) to describe this.

7. How do you as a carer or your organization assess a child's ongoing and changing needs in relation to what you are aiming to achieve?

8. Are there ways this could be developed and perhaps improved?

CHAPTER 11

A New Beginning

An end often implies a new beginning and this is especially so for a child who has reached the stage of recovery. In internalizing her attachments and consolidating her emotional development, she can now move to her next placement, which for most children will be within a family.

Change, loss and leaving are facts of human life and a leaving of any kind may evoke in us feelings which stem from our experience of loss in infancy. For some, this will be comforting because what experience has taught is that loss can bring with it new and loving relationships, that losses are not irreparable, or that they can be survived. For traumatized children, however, change and loss may have been inextricably bound up with being abandoned and rejected, with being sent away and with being unloved and unwanted. This may apply not only to their experience of family life (with carers, where abuse may also have been part of their experience) but perhaps too within the very system that seeks to rescue them. Very often traumatized children are moved from one placement to another with very little planning or preparation and very little understanding on the child's part of why this is happening. They may go from one new family to another, with one more hope dashed in favour of the next, until perhaps the thought of hope is extinguished. These children's fears may be based on a real experience of being forgotten and replaced by others.

The frequent association of endings with a sudden separation is not how a recovered child, at the end of an integrated treatment programme, should experience her next move. The ending for this child is well summed up by Dyke (1984):

122

A perfect ending is not imposed but arrived at. It involves a complete experience of loss, and that which is lost needs to be mourned. It comes out of the acknowledgement of both a good experience having been had, but also the need to move on in order to grow. In the sadness of loss the good object is not attacked but is introjected, that is, taken inside oneself, so that the memory and ability to re-experience it is safely inside to sustain one. (pp.52–53)

The making of the ending

The ending of a placement is therefore in itself a vital part of treatment. As with the beginnings of a placement, the ending has the potential to affirm the child's inner working model. This could be an opportunity to consolidate positively the child's experience of treatment and her reworked model, but it is also a time which runs the risk of undoing the development achieved. At any point of change it is expected that there will be a period of regression and earlier coping mechanisms and defences displayed. Common 'symptoms' include a return to helplessness or a desperate need to control and be self-reliant; or there may be displays of anger leading to verbal or physical attack, self-harm, stealing or obsessive behaviours. However, such displays are generally temporary and less intense than before treatment. The children are usually able to respond to the intervention of carers and draw upon their established relationships and new communication skills, transferring feelings to words.

However, if the process of making an ending is handled without sensitivity and due care, or is felt to be unplanned and forced, a child's anxiety may become overwhelming and her defences reawakened to such a degree that she is unable to hold on to the goodness of what is being left behind. Dyke (1984) warns that 'an ending over which one has no control, and which one is not ready for, can precipitate one into a kind of anti-mourning' (p.57).

Thus, endings need to be positive but those caring for the child need to remember that they are complex. The child is leaving behind the relationships, routines and processes in her therapy, and life story work and home. She is going to a new home, probably a new family, she will be mixing with new people and she may often be moving school – itself difficult enough for healthy children. Of course, what the child has achieved through her treatment – the new sense of self, the ability to relate more positively with others, greater insight and self-understanding, developing self-esteem, and so on – helps to equip her for these changes, but that does not mean they are easily achieved. Transition itself is a word which implies a gradual process, a hopefully smooth moving from one situation to another, creating seamlessness, rather than sudden sharp breaks. Transition can also mean that endings and beginnings overlap or run parallel for a time.

If, as we said at the beginning of this chapter, an end often implies a new beginning, it is also the case that what has gone before remains; it is a part of the child's self, life and experience and she takes it to the next stage of her life. This allows her to look back on real achievement, growth and maturity. What treatment has done is to help the child face and absorb her past, to come through it and past it, and so prepare her for this next phase.

Those working with the child at this time would do well to remember how what may be to most of us very small and common things have now been achieved at great cost to the child and will thus mean a great deal to her. Rymaszewska and Philpot (2006) remind us of this when they say:

> For example, she is now able to invite a hug from the therapist and other adults. This is no small thing when she has been conditioned, through past experience, to regard gestures of apparent affection as laden with sexual potential or threat, when adults were people whose motives were self-interested, when being with them meant having sex with them, and when 'love' was not something which was enhancing and affirming but involved pain, shame, confusion, and destructiveness. (p.126)

For the child the ending is significant and the new beginning is something suffused with potential. She will have mixed feelings about the end and be apprehensive about the future. This may be reflected in the feelings of the recovery team: they will know what she has been through, what she has had to do to get where she is now, and they may foresee difficulties ahead for her because life itself is difficult. But they will also know – and can communicate this to her – that there are others who will help her, on whom she can rely, not least her new family. She can be reassured that she is now more able to receive and accept through her developing ability to trust others, to know that their motives are not hidden, and that when they offer help, either explicitly or implicitly, it is genuine. Destructive relationships can be replaced by constructive ones where, in time, the child too can learn to give, as she has learned to in treatment.

The assessment of a child's recovery is fundamental to the planning of her moving on. There are questions to be asked. What has been the child's progress? What healing has taken place? How different is the child who is leaving from the child who entered treatment? What needs to be done so that she can extend her recovery and growth (itself an implication that what happens in ending is part of the treatment)? Will there be any further contact and if so who with? Who are the significant people in her future life and what is the best way of ensuring that they can help her as best they can? Will she be living with other children (most likely, yes) and how will they be prepared to receive into their home a new member of the family?

Family placement is a good example of where the overlap of ending and beginning already referred to can be seen. It is when there is waiting and introductions, where recovery continues through endings and transitions. It is essential that the child is ready for placement and the recovery team and others work to ensure that the transition to the new family is smooth and secure and, importantly, that the child feels safe.

All members of the recovery team are responsible for the child's ending process and transition to her new placement. They will need to plan and prepare themselves and the child, physically and emotionally. Making use of their supervision, consultants and team meetings will support this process and enable them to process their own feelings, thus enabling them to process those of the child.

As we suggested earlier, traumatized children frequently suffer multiple placements. For many children the need for a specialist placement is only identified following placement breakdowns linked to an increase in intensity and frequency of presenting high-risk behaviours; breakdowns which are likely to confirm a child's view of placements and relationships as transient, unreliable and often abusive. As a result it is commonplace that a child who knows from experience that she is likely to be moved will not invest emotionally in her next placement. The move for a recovered child to a family is one with the potential either to confirm her newly developed belief that relationships may be trusted or, unfortunately, to reaffirm her earlier view of them as untrustworthy and short lived. It is therefore essential that the selection and matching process of a family ensures that the placement is permanent. Moves through placement are damaging for any child, but for a child who has come through treatment they can start to unravel some of the good that has been achieved.

We have referred to the strengths and insights which the recovered child will have acquired. However, it is necessary to remember too that she is still an emotionally fragile child. The secure base that she leaves to join a new family has been time limited and soon she will need intense support during this transition period. Unlike the new family, the child's recovery team are able to use their experience of the child to date to recognize signs of anxiety and stress despite perhaps her outward appearances to the contrary.

A characteristic of children at this time may be that what they say may not be what they think. Anxiety may be covered up and while children may not voice reservations explicitly, they may say things which indicate what lies beneath the surface. For example, a child could spend a day with a foster family with whom it had been suggested that she may live. She may feel uneasy about this but rather than express this openly, she may fix on details – she didn't like the food she was given or she may criticize the way the house is decorated.

In such situations, the recovery team will be handling the child's ambivalent feelings, worries, anxieties and fantasies, helping her to resolve the conflicts she may feel about leaving, letting go and developing new relationships.

Katie: Helping to create your own future

Between the ages of 7 and 12 Katie had moved 28 times. As she arrived at yet another place, with the black bin liners containing all her worldly goods, investing in new relationships came to seem increasingly meaningless. What was planned to be her last residential placement was in a therapeutic setting.

Initially she found the structure, containment and genuine care difficult to cope with. The concept of care was too invasive for her to manage. She had been rejected by her mother and countless other adults and carers and therefore felt unlovable, undeserving and worthless. She tried desperately to create a dysfunctional atmosphere and a barrier to keep carers and others of her age away.

The constant care she received eventually allowed her to make positive relationships and progress. While in her residential placement she confided this was the best place she had ever been and she did not want to leave.

As Katie made positive attachments her behaviour improved and she was able to look forward rather than be weighed down by the past. It became evident that the plan for her future needed to be accomplished: a move from the residential environment to a long-term family placement.

She had always been involved when her future needs were discussed. When it became obvious that a move was imminent she became overtly distressed and regressed, and she attempted to destroy the numerous relationships she had formed. Katie alternated between wanting to go immediately and acting as if she was not ready to go. Her carer had to remain focused on the task of helping her move forward. This presented new challenges for those caring for her as they wanted on the one hand to keep her – she was doing so well – yet on the other understanding the need for the child to leave and continue her growth towards maturity.

Over a planned and extended period Katie was introduced to a practice family, that is a family recruited and trained to work to give a child the opportunity of experiencing the dynamics of a healthy family atmosphere, but who would not become her foster carers. They would visit the house, talk to her and take her out on trips. They would celebrate events such as birthdays with her. At times Katie's fears and anxieties would surface and her behaviour would become quite challenging as she tested her ability to cope and function in such a setting and that of the adults to think about her needs and feelings.

Plans were discussed and made which involved her prospective foster carers, the practice family, and other significant adults.

> Work with Katie continued to allow her to talk through her experiences, fears and anxieties about moving to a new home.
>
> Being worked with like this, Katie was able to discuss how she would want to leave in a positive way. But this also allowed her and her key carer to disengage from one another positively and so symbolize how a good parent can let go.

Moving to placement

The process whereby a child is introduced to her new carers is critical. A rushed introduction which creates momentum and a sense of lack of control is not helpful. Reflection and rehearsal have a place before momentum. Reflection and rehearsal are key words when there is talk of movement and momentum says Byrne (2000), and while she is writing about adoption her principles equally apply to long-term fostering placements.

An introduction lasting 8 to 12 weeks allows appropriate endings, therapeutic closure and time for 'excitement' – a child's initial pleasure at the possibility of a 'forever' family – withdrawal, which is handled by the recovery team, and resolution: leaving the old home and arriving in the new one.

Introductions are not only about introductions to the new family, but also about saying goodbyes. They involve the emotional transfer of attachment from the secure base of the residential home and therapeutic parenting team. As described in the admissions process (see Chapter 6) the aim is to have the child 'claimed' as in attachment theory. The child is being given permission to move physically (by the recovery team, social worker, school, friends and family); emotionally (by herself and by feeling strong and confident); and therapeutically (by having closure of the current therapeutic process).

These are not processes to be rushed and they do not just happen. As we have said, the recovery team needs to talk with the children about their feelings, worries and anxieties. Equally, the family placement team needs to talk about the same subjects with the new family. It is sometimes tempting in this process to deny the less positive feelings about the move for fear that this would somehow prevent it from happening. However, the reverse is often the case: unspoken fears and anxieties denied will usually be acted out and presented in less manageable forms which may then lead to a rejection by either party.

The child's home is where the process of the move begins. As with the earlier admission process, the child is visited by her future family at her present home. At first the meetings fully involve the child's key carer but then move to being just the child and the new family. Similarly, in tandem with this are visits of increasing duration to the new family home. When the child is with the new family, opportunities can be provided for her to rehearse undertaking regular routines and activity in this new setting, for example going to school. Visits before placement provide opportunities for the child to transfer to her new home emotionally and physically. It is something which will initiate the grieving process and diminish fears and worries for the future.

The child will look to her key carer and recovery team for reassurance about the pending move and the new family. It is important, therefore, that she is able to observe positive interactions and communications between them. Having built a trusting and reliable relationship with the key carer, she will look for positive and negative cues to confirm her own anxieties or excitement. Important here is the key carer's ability to gradually 'hand over' the child to the care and authority of the new family. One way in which this can symbolically take place is by the 'handing over' of the child's life story book. In this way the key carer can demonstrate to the child that he believes that the new family can welcome and look after the 'whole' of her, her past as well as her present and future. The new family then have the opportunity to confirm their ability and wish to do so.

Throughout the transition period it is important to review the progress made and the pace of activity. It may be necessary to slow things down or offer additional support and opportunities for everyone to reflect on what is happening and to process the many feelings aroused by the move. Equally important is a recognition that the grieving process does not suddenly end when something new comes along. Careful attention needs to be paid to planning the child's continuing contact with significant members of the recovery team. Planning the calendar year ahead can highlight important events and dates for the child who would perhaps benefit from some sort of contact like birthdays, Christmas and anniversaries. Any of these may trigger intense feelings and a simple card or telephone call could help the child manage these reoccurring emotions. However, it is essential this kind of contact is planned beforehand and the child expects it, as unplanned individual acts of contact may be more about an inability to let go rather than assist in letting go.

Thus, the child has now lived through a kaleidoscope of experiences where treatment has enabled her to overcome the distortion which abuse has wrought on her life, outlook and perceptions. She is no longer imprisoned by her past and she has reached her new beginning.

Exercises

1. Try to recall a time when you have started something new, perhaps a new job, a new relationship.

2. What preparation did you undertake for this?

3. What preparation do you think others undertook?

4. Can you recall how you felt about this new start?

5. Reflecting on some of the themes presented in this book imagine you are planning a transition for a child.

6. What key events or elements would you build into the plan?

7. List the range of emotions which may be present for: the child, the new carers, new siblings, the current carers, and the current children's group.

8. What ideas do you have about how these emotions could be thought about within your organization or care setting?

Notes

1. Kieran O'Hagan (2006) has noted dramatic increases in the use of neglect as a category in child abuse registrations. However, he suggests that this stems from a lack of clarity in the definition of abuse and neglect and 'a convenient avoidance of the reality of specific types of abuse perpetuated against children'.

2. Fifteen is given here as being the year below that of sexual consent. A child or young person aged 15 and under cannot by law consent to sex. Obviously, above the age of 16 there is such a thing as non-consensual sex and people of any age can be sexually abused.

3. ChildLine's estimate may well be correct, but it is wise to remember that girls outnumber boys by a ratio of 1:4 in calling the helpline on almost any subject, something which may skew the figures. However, given that males are less likely to report sexual abuse anyway, it is likely that other estimates would indicate the same proportions.

4. For a discussion of complicated family and other relationships for abused children and how they may understand them, see Rose and Philpot (2005).

5. Therapeutic parenting, as described in this book, is practised as part of an integrated approach which also involves life story work and therapy. For a detailed description of these two methods and how all three work together see Rose and Philpot (2005) and Rymaszewska and Philpot (2006).

6. For the work of Neill and Lane see Croall (1983) and Wills (1964), as well as Neill and Lane's own books.

7. Introjection is the process by which the functions of an external object are taken over by its mental representation. The object 'out there' is replaced by an imagined object 'inside'. What results is called the introject or the introjected object. As a defence introjection diminishes separation anxiety; as a developmental process it makes the subject increasingly autonomous.

8. This section draws on Tomlinson (2004).

References

Adoption UK (2000) *Making Sense of Attachments in Adoptive and Foster Families*. Banbury: Adoption UK.

Alvarez, A. (1992) *Live Company: Psychoanalytic Psychotherapy with Autistic, Borderline, Deprived and Abused Children*. London: Routledge.

Archer, C. (2003) 'Weft and warp: Developmental impact of trauma and implications for healing.' In C. Archer and A. Burnell (eds) *Trauma, Attachment and Family Permanence: Fear Can Stop You Loving*. London: Jessica Kingsley Publishers.

Aynsley-Green, A. (2005) 'Understanding opportunities for improving the lives of children and young people.' YoungMinds Annual Lecture, London, 10 November.

Balbernie, R. (1973) 'The management of an evolving care system.' In J. Hunter and F.R. Ainsworth (eds) *Residential Establishments*. Dundee: University of Dundee.

Balbernie, R (1989) 'Looking at what professional carers do: The therapeutic context and conditions of change.' *Maladjustment and Therapeutic Education 7*, 1, Spring.

Bateman, A., Brown, D. and Pedder, J. (2000) *Introduction to Psychotherapy: An Outline of Psychodynamic Principles and Practice*, 3rd edn. London: Brunner-Routledge.

Bettelheim, B. (1950) 'Food: The great socializer.' In B. Bettelheim *Love is Not Enough: The Treatment of Emotionally Disturbed Children*. London: Free Press.

Bowlby, J. (1969) *Attachment*. London: Hogarth Press.

Bowlby, J. (1973–1980) *Attachment Trilogy: Volumes 1–111*. London: Hogarth Press.

Bowlby, J. (1979) *The Making and Breaking of Affectional Bonds*. London: Tavistock.

Brown, J.L. (undated) 'Routines.' Unpublished paper.

Burnell, A. and Archer, C. (2003) 'Setting up the loom: Attachment theory revisited.' In C. Archer and A. Burnell (eds) *Trauma, Attachment and Family Permanence: Fear Can Stop You Loving*. London: Jessica Kingsley Publishers.

Butlin, E. (1973) 'Institutionalisation, management structure and therapy in residential work with emotionally disturbed children.' *British Journal of Social Work 5*, 3, 283–295.

Byrne, S. (2000) *Linking and Introductions: Helping Children Join Adoptive Families*. London: BAAF Adoption and Fostering.

Cairns, K. (2002) *Attachment, Trauma and Resilience: Therapeutic Caring for Children*. London: BAAF Adoption and Fostering.

Canham, H. (1998) 'Growing up in residential care.' *Journal of Social Work Practice 12*, 1, 66.

Carter, J. (2003) 'The meaning of good experience.' In A. Ward, K. Kasinski, J. Pooley and A. Worthington (eds) *Therapeutic Communities for Children and Young People*. London: Jessica Kingsley Publishers.

ChildLine (2003) *Annual Report.* London: ChildLine.

Cohen, D. (2002) *How the Child's Mind Develops.* Hove: Brunner-Routledge.

Copley, B. and Forryan, B. (1987) *Therapeutic Work with Children and Young People.* London: Robert Royce.

Croall, J. (1983) *Neill of Summerhill: The Permanent Rebel.* London: Ark.

Daws, D. (1993) *Through the Night: Helping Parents and Sleepless Infants.* London: Free Association Books.

Department of Health (2003) *Safeguarding Children: What to Do if You Are Worried a Child is Being Abused.* London: Department of Health.

Department of Health and Social Services (1974) *Report of the Enquiry into the Care and Supervision Provided in Relation to Maria Colwell.* London: HMSO.

Dockar-Drysdale, B. (1968) *Therapy and Consultation in Child Care.* London: Longman.

Dockar-Drysdale, B. (1990a) 'The problem of making adaptation to the needs of the individual child in the group.' In B. Dockar-Drysdale *The Provision of Primary Experience: Winnicottian Work with Children and Adolescents.* London: Free Association Books.

Dockar-Drysdale, B. (1990b) *The Provision of Primary Experience: Winnicottian Work with Children and Adolescents.* London: Free Association Books.

Dyke, S.L. (1984) 'Letting go: A psychotherapist's view of endings.' *Journal of Maladjustment and Therapeutic Education 2*, 1, 52–53.

Erikson, E. (1950) *Childhood and Society.* New York: Norton.

Fahlberg, V.I. (1994) *A Child's Journey Through Placement.* London: BAAF Adoption and Fostering.

Flynn, D. (1998) 'In-patient work in a therapeutic community.' In M. Lanyado and A. Horne (eds) *The Handbook of Child and Adolescent Psychotherapy: Psychoanalytic Approaches.* London: Routledge.

The Guardian (2005) 'Vital statistics: The world of women in numbers', 19 May.

Howe, D. (2000) 'Attachment theory.' In M. Davies (ed.) *The Blackwell Encyclopaedia of Social Work.* Oxford: Blackwell.

Hunter, M. (2001) *Psychotherapy with Young People in Care: Lost and Found.* Hove: Brunner-Routledge.

James, B. (1994) *Handbook for Treatment of Attachment-Trauma Problems in Children.* New York: Free Press.

Karr-Morse, R. and Wiley, M. (1997) *Ghosts from the Nursery: Tracing the Roots of Violence.* New York: Atlantic Monthly Press.

Kennard, D. (1998) *An Introduction to Therapeutic Communities,* 2nd edn. London: Jessica Kingsley Publishers.

Kubler-Ross, E. (1970) *On Death and Dying.* London: Tavistock.

Lanyado, M. (1981) '"United we stand…?" Stress in residential work with disturbed children.' *Maladjustment and Therapeutic Education 7*, 3, 136–146.

Lanyado, M. (1991) 'On creating a psychotherapeutic space.' *British Journal of Social Work 5*, 1, 136–146.

Lanyado, M. (2000) 'Daring to try again: The hope and pain of forming new attachment.' Paper given to the Annual Care and Treatment Inset Conference of the Charterhouse Group of Therapeutic Communities, 20 September.

Lanyado, M. (2003) 'The roots of mental health: Emotional development and the caring environment.' In A. Ward, K. Kasinski, J. Pooley and A. Worthington (eds) *Therapeutic Communities for Children and Young People.* London: Jessica Kingsley Publishers.

Leiper, R. and Maltby, M. (2004) *The Psychodynamic Approach to Therapeutic Change.* London: Sage.

Lucas, M. (1992) 'Special things: The management of an individual provision within a group care setting for emotionally disturbed children.' *Therapeutic Communities 13*, 4.

Maginn, C. (2006) 'Pillar talk.' *Community Care*, 16–22 March.

Maier, H.W. (1985) 'Primary care in secondary settings: Inherent strains.' In F.L. Fulcher and F. Ainsworth (eds) *Group Care Practice with Children.* London: Tavistock.

Miller, A. (1995) *The Drama of Being a Child*, 2nd edn. London: Virago.

O'Hagan, K. (2006) 'Just call it abuse.' *Community Care*, 15–19 January.

Philpot, T. (1994) *Action for Children: The Story of Britain's Foremost Children's Charity.* Oxford: Lion.

Plotnikoff, J. and Wolfson, R. (2005) *In their Own Words: The Experiences of 50 Young Witnesses in Criminal Proceedings.* London: NSPCC.

Preston-Shoot, M. and Agass, D. (1990) *Making Sense of Social Work: Psychodynamics, Systems and Practice.* London: Macmillan.

Richardson, A. and Montgomery, P. (2005) 'The Oxford–Durham study: A randomised controlled trial of dietary supplementation with fatty acids in children with developmental co-ordination disorder.' *Pediatrics 115*, 1300–1366.

Rose, M. (1987) 'The function of food in residential treatment.' *Journal of Adolescence 10*, 149–162.

Rose, M. (2002) 'Children and adolescents: The renaissance of heart and mind.' In P. Campling and R. Haigh (eds) *Therapeutic Communities: Past, Present and Future*, 2nd edn. London: Jessica Kingsley Publishers.

Rose, R. and Philpot, T. (2005) *The Child's Own Story: Life Story Work with Traumatized Children.* London: Jessica Kingsley Publishers.

Rymaskewska, J. and Philpot, T. (2006) *Reaching the Vulnerable Child: Therapy with Traumatized Children.* London: Jessica Kingsley Publishers.

Sanderson, C. (2004) *The Seduction of Children: Empowering Parents and Teachers to Protect Children from Child Sexual Abuse.* London: Jessica Kingsley Publishers.

Schmidt Neven, R. (1997) *Emotional Milestones from Birth to Adulthood: A Psychodynamic Approach.* London: Jessica Kingsley Publishers.

Schore, A. (1994) *After Regulation and the Origin of the Self.* Hillsdale, NJ: Lawrence Erlbaum Associates, Inc.

Simmonds, J. (1988) 'Thinking about feelings in group care.' In G. Pearson, J. Treseder and M. Yelloly (eds) *Social Work and the Legacy of Freud.* Basingstoke: Macmillan.

Solomon, J. and George, C. (1999) 'The place of disorganisation in attachment theory: Linking classic observations with contemporary findings.' In J. Solomon and C. George (eds) *Attachment Disorganisation.* New York: Guilford Press.

Tomlinson, P. (2004) *Therapeutic Approaches to Work with Traumatized Children and Young People: Theory and Practice.* London: Jessica Kingsley Publishers.

Wagner, G. (1980) *Barnardo.* London: Eyre and Spottiswoode.

Walsh, M. (2002) '24 Outcomes for recovery' in M. Walsh and P. Tomlinson (eds) *The SACCS Recovery Programme.* Unpublished.

Ward, A. (2003) 'The core framework.' In A. Ward, K. Kasinski, J. Pooley and A. Worthington (eds) *Therapeutic Communities for Children and Young People.* London: Jessica Kingsley Publishers.

Ward, A. (2004) 'Assessing and meeting children's emotional needs.' Unpublished lecture notes for therapeutic childcare study day, University of Reading.

Ward, A., Kasinski, K., Pooley, J. and Worthington, A. (2003) 'Management and development. Introduction.' In A. Ward, K. Kasinski, J. Pooley and A. Worthington (eds) *Therapeutic Communities for Children and Young People.* London: Jessica Kingsley Publishers.

Whitwell, J. (1994) 'Staying alive: Is there a future for long-term psychotherapeutic child care?' *Therapeutic Communities 15,* 2.

Wills, D.W. (1964) *Homer Lane: A Biography.* London: Allen & Unwin.

Wilson, P. (2003) 'Consultation and supervision.' In A. Ward, K. Kasinski, J. Pooley and A. Worthington (eds) *Therapeutic Communities for Children and Young People.* London: Jessica Kingsley Publishers.

Winnicott, D.W. (1990) *The Maturational Processes and the Facilitating Environment.* London: Karnac (first published 1960).

Winnicott, D.W. (1992) *Through Paediatrics to Psycho-analysis.* London: Karnac (first published 1975).

YoungMinds (2004) *Mental Health in Infancy.* London: YoungMinds.

Ziegler, D. (2002) *Traumatic Experience and the Brain: A Handbook for Understanding and Treating Those Traumatized as Children.* Phoenix: Acacia Publishing.

The Story of SACCS

In the 1960s and 1970s professionals focused on the physical abuse (or what was called the battered baby syndrome) and neglect of children. Sexual abuse only began to gain attention in the early 1980s.

The challenge then for social workers in child protection was to deal with this new phenomenon as part of everyday practice. They had to develop new skills to communicate with children on a subject which they, as adults, had difficulty with, that is talking about sex and their own sexuality, and moreover doing this in a way that could withstand in court the rigours of legal scrutiny.

It was at this point that Mary Walsh, now chief executive of SACCS, got together with a local authority colleague, Madge Bray, who was working to help disturbed children communicate by using toys. Together they looked at how they could adapt the use of the toy box to help this very vulnerable group of children communicate their distress, especially about the abuse they had suffered. Above all, they wanted to give children a voice in decisions that would be made about them, particularly in court.

SACCS comes into being

Working within the culture of uncertainty and confusion that prevailed at the time, Mary Walsh and Madge Bray became disenchanted with the lack of time and resources available to do this work properly. They saw no alternative: in January 1987 they took it upon themselves to meet the profound needs of the deeply traumatized children whom they were seeing every day and who found themselves effectively lost and without any influence on their futures.

SACCS came into being in Madge Bray's back bedroom – the typewriter had to be unplugged to use the photocopier! Demand for the venture on which they were now embarked soon became apparent. They were inundated with requests to see children and help them to communicate about their distress. Mary Walsh and Madge Bray worked with children all over the country, helping them to tell their stories, giving comfort and allowing them to express their pain. They also acted as advocates for children in court and other decision-making bodies, and as case consultants to local authorities. Through this process, as expected, they began to notice that many of the children were changing and beginning to find some resolution to their difficulties.

They also became aware that there were some very small children who because of what had happened to them were either too eroticized or too disturbed to be placed in foster care. Many foster carers who were not prepared or trained to deal with very challenging situations day to day would quickly become weighed down by the child's sexualized behaviour and the placement would break down. The real cause of these breakdowns was never acknowledged and therefore never dealt with. In time these children were labelled as unfosterable and placed in residential care along with much older children and young people.

Leaps and Bounds

The heartbreak of watching this happen to three-, four- and five-year-old children was unacceptable. The need was to be able to hold the children and their behaviour lovingly, while they were helped to understand and deal with the root cause of their behaviour. The result was the setting up of Leaps and Bounds, the first SACCS residential care provision.

The birth was a long and difficult one, but after three years the first house, Hopscotch, was opened. It filled up immediately and the children were cared for by staff trained to understand the issues and encouraged to put love into everything they did. Many of the children placed in Leaps and Bounds had experienced numerous placement breakdowns. Some had been placed for adoption that had subsequently failed. Most had incoherent life histories. Some had lost touch with members of their family and one child, incredibly, had acquired the wrong name. The great need was to find all of this information that was lost in the system, and so the life story service came into existence, to help to piece together the fabric of the children's lives and give them back their own identity.

In addition, a team of professional play therapists was engaged to work with the children at Hopscotch, and subsequently at the new houses – Somersault, Cartwheel, Handstand, Leapfrog, and others – while continuing to bring the special SACCS approach to children who were not in residential care.

Within SACCS, all those charged with responsibility for the well-being of the child were (and are) expected to share information with each other, so that the whole team holds the child's reality and care.

Find Us, Keep Us

The expectation at SACCS was that when children had come to terms with what had happened to them and were ready to move on, their local authorities would find foster families for them. This proved not to be the case in many instances, and children who had worked hard to recover and desperately wanted to be part of a family would have their hopes dashed. As a result their behaviour deteriorated. It was extremely difficult to watch this happening, especially as the next part of the work needed to be done within a family.

Leaps and Bounds was never intended to become a permanent placement for the children, so looking for potential foster families and training them to care for this very challenging and vulnerable group of children became the responsibility of a new part of SACCS which was founded – Find Us, Keep Us, the fostering and family placement arm of the organization.

Flying Colours

In 1997 Flying Colours was opened. It was a new project designed to meet the needs of young adolescents. Often these were children who had been traumatized when they were very young, but had only just started to talk about it. As a therapist, Mary Walsh had worked with many such young people, who were not being held in a safe and contained environment. She knew that they often ran away when feelings overwhelmed them, and sometimes ended up living hand to mouth on inner city streets, involved in prostitution, drug taking, and worse. Flying Colours offered these young people the same loving and nurturing therapeutic care as the younger children in Leaps and Bounds, while at the same time meeting their different developmental needs.

SACCS Care

In 2003, a major rationalization was undertaken to integrate all of the SACCS services which had evolved since the organization's early days. A new company, SACCS Care, was formed, with an organizational focus on the parenting aspect of therapeutic care. This is arguably the most important job carried out with children, some of whom have similar developmental profiles to the most dangerous adults in our society. SACCS believes that unless this issue is addressed properly, traumatized children cannot have a positive experience of parenting, and when the time comes will be unable to parent their own children appropriately.

Today and tomorrow

SACCS Care is differentiated by a unique integrated model of therapeutic parenting, play therapy, life story work and education support individually tailored to meet children's needs, coupled with a fostering service for those who are ready to move to a family.

At the time of writing, SACCS Care is a growing Midlands-based organization looking after 70 children and employing 175 professional care staff and managers. The SACCS model is underpinned by a complex structure of practice training and clinical supervision, and these standards of excellence have positioned the organization as a national leader in therapeutic care and recovery.

There are many children outside SACCS struggling with the enormous trauma caused by abuse and neglect, children whose experience has taught them that families are dangerous places in which to live. SACCS believes that every child has a right to the expert therapeutic care which can help them to recover from their emotional injuries, but for these children the specialist services they require are often not available.

The next step in the SACCS story will be the establishment of a college to train carers in the SACCS model. The wider implications are that this training can ultimately inform practice with traumatized children everywhere.

The Authors

Billy Pughe is Operations Director of SACCS Care Ltd, a UKCP-registered group analyst and a member of the Institute of Group Analysis. Originally trained as a teacher, she began her career teaching at Kilworthy House, a therapeutic community for children and young people. Gaining a postgraduate Diploma in Therapeutic Child Care at Reading University, she continued her career in two further communities, The Caldecott and The Cotswold, and within the NHS as a group therapist within both children and adult mental health services.

Terry Philpot is a journalist and writer and is a contributor to, among others, *The Tablet*, *The Guardian* and *Times Higher Education Supplement*. He was formerly editor of *Community Care*. He has written and edited several books, the latest of which are (with Anthony Douglas) *Adoption: Changing Families, Changing Times* (2002), (with Julia Feast) *Searching Questions. Identity, Origins and Adoption* (2003), (with Clive Sellick and June Thoburn) *What Works in Foster Care and Adoption?* (2004), (with Richard Rose) *The Child's Own Story. Life Story Work with Traumatized Children* (2004), and (with Janie Rymaszewska) *Reaching the Vulnerable Child. Therapy with Traumatized Children* (2006). He has also published reports on private fostering, kinship care and residential care for older people run by the Catholic Church. He is a trustee of the Centre for Policy on Ageing, and the Social Care Institute for Excellence and was, until 2006, a trustee of Rainer. He has won several awards for journalism.

Subject Index

Author Index

Adoption UK 22
Agass, D. 38, 48–9
Alvarez, A. 15, 120–1
Archer, C. 23
Aynsley-Green, A. 11,
    32–3

Balbernie, R. 100–1
Bateman, A. 38
Bettelheim, B. 91
Bowlby, J. 21, 38, 40
Brown, D. 38
Brown, J.L. 64, 88
Burnell, A. 23
Butlin, E. 47
Byrne, S. 128

Cairns, K. 25, 26, 36
Canham, H. 42
Carter, J. 87
ChildLine 15
Cohen, D. 24
Copley, B. 48
Croall, J. 131

Daws, D. 63
Department of Health 13
Dockar-Drysdale, B. 34,
    35, 98, 103, 108
Dyke, S.L. 122, 123

Erikson, E. 39

Fahlberg, V.I. 112
Flynn, D. 120
Forryan, B. 48

George, C. 23
Guardian 13

Howe, D. 21, 23
Hunter, M. 17, 18

James, B. 26–7, 29

Karr-Morse, R. 25
Kennard, D. 41, 42
Kubler-Ross, E. 18

Lanyado, M. 22, 41, 52,
    102
Leiper, R. 39
Lucas, M. 107–8

Maginn, C. 33, 34
Maier, H.W. 108
Maltby, M. 39
Miller, A. 11, 12
Montgomery, P. 89

O'Hagan, K. 131

Pedder, J. 38
Philpot, T. 13, 18, 97,
    112, 119, 124, 131
Plotnikoff, J. 19
Preston-Shoot, M. 38,
    48–9

Richardson, A. 89
Rose, M. 43, 44, 87
Rose, R. 97, 112, 119,
    131
Rymaskewska, J. 18

Sanderson, C. 14
Schmidt Neven, R. 40
Schore, A. 23
Simmonds, J. 47
Solomon, J. 23

Tomlinson, P. 49, 70, 100,
    103

Wagner, G. 13
Ward, A. 40, 47, 111
Whitwell, J. 51–2
Wiley, M. 25
Wills, D.W. 131
Wilson, P. 48
Winnicott, D.W. 38, 40,
    78, 97–8
Wolfson, R. 19

YoungMinds 23–4

Ziegler, D. 26, 30